Physical Science: Concepts in Action
Math Skills and Problem Solving Workbook

Contents

Math Skills and
Problem Solving Workbook

Prentice Hall
Physical
Science
Concepts in Action
With Earth and Space Science

PEARSON

Prentice
Hall

Boston, Massachusetts
Upper Saddle River, New Jersey

Math Skills and
Problem Solving Workbook

Prentice Hall
Physical
Science
Concepts in Action
With Earth and Space Science

ISBN 0-13-125889-3

11 12 13 14 15   12 11 10 09

Section 1.3 Measurement

(pages 14–21)

Math Skills *Using Scientific Notation*

Content and Vocabulary Support

Writing Numbers in Scientific Notation

Scientific notation is a way of writing numbers that are very large or very small. It makes the numbers easier to work with by eliminating most of the zeroes. In scientific notation, a number is expressed as the product of a number from 1 to 10 and 10 raised to a power. For example, 2,000,000 (2 million) is written as 2.0×10^6. To change 2,000,000 to 2.0, the decimal point was moved six places to the left. Because the decimal point was moved six places, the power of 10 is 6.

To change a very small number (less than one) to scientific notation, you follow the same steps, except the decimal point is moved to the right. This makes the exponent a negative number. For example, 0.000002 (2 millionths) is written as 2.0×10^{-6}.

To change a number from scientific notation to standard notation, you follow the same steps in reverse order. Based on the value and sign of the exponent, write the correct number of zeroes before or after the number. Then, move the decimal point the same number of places to the left or right.

Arithmetic with Numbers in Scientific Notation

You can add and subtract numbers in scientific notation if they are raised to the same power of 10. For example:

$$(1.0 \times 10^4) + (2.2 \times 10^4) = 3.2 \times 10^4$$

You can multiply or divide any numbers in scientific notation. To multiply, first multiply the two numbers that appear before the multiplication signs. Then, add the two exponents. For example:

$$(3.1 \times 10^8) \times (2.0 \times 10^3) = (3.1 \times 2.0) \times 10^{(8+3)} = 6.2 \times 10^{11}$$

To divide, first divide the two numbers that appear before the multiplication signs. Then, subtract the two exponents. For example:

$$\frac{(4.2 \times 10^{12})}{(2.0 \times 10^3)} = \frac{4.2}{2.0} \times 10^{(12-3)} = 2.1 \times 10^9$$

Name _____ Class _____ Date _____

Section 1.3 Measurement

Solved Examples

Example 1: A hydrogen atom has a diameter of 0.00000001 cm. What is the diameter in scientific notation?

Given: Diameter in standard notation = 0.00000001 cm

Unknown: Diameter in scientific notation

Solution: The diameter is 1.0×10^{-8}. The decimal point is moved eight places to the right to change the number to 1.0. The exponent of 10 is therefore negative eight.

Example 2: What is the area of a rectangular playing field that is 5.0×10^3 m wide and 8.0×10^4 m long?

Given: Width (w) = 5.0×10^3 m
Length (l) = 8.0×10^4 m

Unknown: Area (A)

Equation: $A = l \times w$

Solution: $A = (8.0 \times 10^4 \text{ m}) \times (5.0 \times 10^3 \text{ m}) = 40.0 \times 10^7 \text{ m}^2$

Example 3: One side of a microchip has an area of 5×10^{-6} m^2 and a length of 5.0×10^{-3} m. What is its width?

Given: Area (A) = 5.0×10^{-6} m^2
Length (l) = 5.0×10^{-3} m

Unknown: Width (w)

Equation: $w = \dfrac{A}{l}$

Solution: $w = \dfrac{5.0 \times 10^{-6} \text{m}^2}{5.0 \times 10^{-3} \text{m}} = 1.0 \times 10^{-3}$ m

Practice Exercises

Exercise 1: Scientists use the micron as a unit of length for very small objects. A micron is one-millionth of a meter, or 0.000001 m. Write the number of meters in a micron in scientific notation.

Exercise 2: A mountain's elevation above sea level is 9.8×10^3 m. Write the elevation in standard notation.

Exercise 3: A rectangular lake has a width of 6.0×10^3 m and a length of 1.2×10^4 m. What is the area of the lake in scientific notation?

Exercise 4: A rectangular piece of land with an area of 260,000 m^2 is 2,000 m long. Write the area and length in scientific notation, and then find the width.

Exercise 5: One surface of a cut gemstone is rectangular in shape. It is 0.0002 m wide and has an area of 0.000006 m^2. How long is the surface? Do your work in scientific notation.

Chapter 1   Skills for Doing Science

Section 1.4 Presenting Scientific Data
(pages 22–25)

Data Analysis *Organizing Data in Tables and Line Graphs*

Content and Vocabulary Support

Organizing Data

To be the most useful, scientific data should be organized. The simplest way to organize data is in a data table. Often, the data in tables are plotted in graphs, because graphs make it easier to see relationships and trends in the data. Commonly used types of graphs include line graphs, bar graphs, and circle graphs.

Line Graphs

A line graph is a good choice for showing changes in related variables. Generally, values for the manipulated variable are plotted on the horizontal ($x-$) axis, and values for the responding variable are plotted on the vertical ($y-$) axis. When all the data points are plotted, they are connected to form a line.

The steepness of the line is called the **slope**. The slope is calculated with the formula:

$$\text{Slope} = \frac{\text{Rise}}{\text{Run}}$$

Rise is the difference between two y values. Run is the difference between the two corresponding x values. The steeper the line, the greater the slope. The greater the slope, the more the responding variable changes with each change in the manipulated variable. If the slope is positive, both variables change in the same direction. If the slope is negative, the two variables change in opposite directions.

When the ratio of two variables is constant, they have a relationship called a **direct proportion**. For example, if one variable is always twice as great as the other, the two variables are directly proportional. A direct proportion produces a straight-line graph. When the product of two variables is constant, they have a relationship called an **indirect proportion**. For example, The product of speed and time equals distance. If distance is constant, as it is in a race, then speed and time are indirectly proportional. An indirect proportion produces a curved-line graph.

Section 1.4 Presenting Scientific Data

Data

Average temperatures vary by latitude, or distance north or south of the equator. At higher latitudes, the sun's rays are less direct, leading to less heating of Earth's surface. The table shows latitudes and average annual temperatures for several cities in the U.S.

Latitude and Average Annual Temperature for U.S. Cities		
City	*Latitude*	*Average Annual Temperature*
Denver	39° 45 min N	10°C
Houston	29° 58 min N	19°C
Los Angeles	33° 56 min N	18°C
Miami	25° 48 min N	24°C
New York	40° 47 min N	12°C
Portland	45° 36 min N	12°C
San Francisco	37° 37 min N	13°C
Tulsa	36° 12 min N	15°C

At a high school track meet, eight runners competed in the 200-m dash. The graph shows their speeds and finishing times.

Speeds and Finishing Times for 200-m Dash

Questions

1. a. Identifying Identify the city in the table that has the lowest latitude and the city that has the highest latitude. What is the average annual temperature for each city?

_____

_____

b. Graphing If you were going to draw a line graph of the values in the table, which variable would you plot on the *x*-axis and which variable you would plot on the *y*-axis? Explain your choices.

_____

_____

_____

_____

_____

c. Interpreting Data Based on the data in the table, how does average temperature change as latitude increases? How could you reorganize the data in the table to make this relationship more obvious?

_____

_____

_____

_____

_____

2. a. Describing Describe how the responding variable changes as the manipulated variable increases.

_____

_____

_____

b. Applying Concepts Does the graph represent a direct proportion or an inverse proportion?

_____

_____

c. Predicting Use the graph to predict how long it would take a runner to finish the 200-m dash at a speed of 6.5 m/s. At a speed of 8.2 m/s.

_____

_____

Chapter 2   Properties of Matter

Section 2.1 Classifying Matter
(pages 38–44)

Data Analysis *Analyzing Mixtures*

Content and Vocabulary Support

Mixtures

A mixture is a combination of more than one substance. Unlike a **compound**, which always has exactly the same makeup, the composition of a mixture may vary. For example, soil is a mixture of small bits of rocks and minerals and tiny pieces of dead leaves and other organic matter. Most soils contain all of these components but in different proportions. Some soils contain more rocks and minerals, others more organic matter.

Heterogeneous and Homogeneous Mixtures

Mixtures also vary in how evenly their components are distributed. Consider a pot of vegetable soup. One bowl of soup from the pot may contain more carrots and less green beans than another bowl of soup taken from the same pot. This is because the ingredients are not evenly distributed throughout the soup. When the parts of a mixture are noticeably different from one another, it is called a **heterogeneous mixture**. Another example of a heterogeneous mixture is sand on a beach, which is a mixture of different types and sizes of rock and shell particles.

Other mixtures have their components more evenly distributed. As a result, the parts of the mixture are not noticeably different from one another. Such a mixture is called a **homogeneous mixture.** An example of a homogeneous mixture is lemonade. Lemonade is a mixture of water, lemon juice, and sugar. If the lemonade in a pitcher is well mixed, each glass of lemonade poured from the pitcher has about the same composition. You also cannot distinguish the lemon juice, water, and sugar from each other in the mixture, so the lemonade appears to contain only one substance. Another example of a homogenous mixture is sterling silver, which is a mixture of silver and copper.

Name _____ Class _____ Date _____

Section 2.1 Classifying Matter

Data

To reduce lawn care, a landscaper suggests planting part of a public park with a mixture of prairie grasses that need to be cut only once a year. Table 1 shows the composition of two different prairie grass seed mixtures the landscaper is considering.

Table 1. Prairie Grass Seed Mixtures		
Type of Grass Seed (growing conditions)	Mass in Seed Mixture A (g)	Mass in Seed Mixture B (g)
Buffalo grass (sun, dry)	32	181
Indian grass (sun, dry)	78	209
Porcupine grass (sun, dry)	86	86
Prairie cordgrass (sun, dry)	34	129
Rattlesnake grass (shade, wet)	275	35
Silky wild rye (shade, wet)	124	40
Slender wheat grass (sun, dry)	91	166
Sweet grass (sun, wet)	52	49
Switch grass (sun, dry)	38	77
Virginia wild rye (shade, wet)	190	28

Claire has an allergy to monosodium glutamate, and Dillon is on a sodium-restricted diet. Both are trying to decide which brand of canned chicken broth to buy. Table 2 shows the composition of two different brands of broth.

Table 2. Chicken Broth Brands		
Ingredient	Percent by Mass of Brand A	Percent by Mass of Brand B
Water	94.55	95.15
Salt	2.22	0.53
Monosodium glutamate	1.01	0.10
Wheat and soy protein	0.43	1.12
Onion flakes	0.42	0.86
Garlic powder	0.39	0.51
Sugar	0.38	0.15
Spices	0.21	0.32
Powdered cooked chicken	0.15	1.28
Turmeric	0.09	0.08
Disodium inosinate	0.08	0.05
Disodium guanylate	0.07	0.03

Questions

1. a. Identifying In Table 1, identify the type of seeds with the greatest mass in mixture A and in mixture B.

_____

b. Calculating How many grams of seeds in 1,000 grams of mixture A grow in sunny, dry conditions? How many grams of mixture B?

_____

_____

c. Inferring The area where the seeds would be planted is shady and wet. Explain which seed mixture would probably grow better there.

_____

_____

_____

2. a. Identifying In Table 2, identify the brand of chicken broth that contains less monosodium glutamate.

_____

b. Calculating Find the percent of salt and other sodium-containing ingredients in each brand of broth.

_____

_____

c. Concluding Conclude which brand of broth Claire and Dillon should choose.

_____

_____

_____

3. a. Classifying Which type of mixture, seeds or broth, is an example of a heterogeneous mixture? Of a homogeneous mixture? Explain your choices.

_____

_____

_____

b. Applying Concepts Explain why all four mixtures are not compounds.

_____

_____

Chapter 3   States of Matter

Section 3.1 Solids, Liquids, and Gases
(pages 68–74)

> **Data Analysis** *Analyzing States of Matter*

Content and Vocabulary Support

States of Matter

Almost all matter on Earth is in a solid, liquid, or gaseous state. Examples of matter in each state are ice (solid), water (liquid), and water vapor (gas). The major difference between the three states is the degree to which they can change in shape and volume.

Solids

A **solid** has a definite shape and volume. Solid objects such as rocks stay the same even if you try to press them into different shapes or sizes. Solids keep the same shape and volume because their particles vibrate around fixed locations in an orderly arrangement. Other examples of solids include steel and wood.

Liquids

A **liquid** has a definite volume but not a definite shape. Liquids take the same shape as their container. You can pour juice from a square box into a round glass and the juice will change shape to match the container. Liquids change shape because their particles can flow. However, liquids change very little in volume, because forces of attraction between the particles keep them together. Other examples of liquids include syrup and milk.

Gases

A **gas** has neither a definite shape nor a definite volume. Gases take both the shape and the volume of their container. For example, you can heat the air in a balloon to make it increase in volume, or you can squeeze a balloon to make the air inside take a different shape. Gases can change both shape and volume because their particles are in constant, random motion and can move far apart from one another. This allows a gas to fill a container of any shape or size. In addition to air, other gases include helium and carbon dioxide.

Other States of Matter

At extremely high and low temperatures, matter can in exist in other states. On the sun and other stars, where temperatures are very high, most matter exists in a state called *plasma*. Where temperatures are very low, matter exists in a state called a *Bose-Einstein condensate*.

Section 3.1 Solids, Liquids, and Gases

Data

When molecules of a gas heat up, they gain energy and increase in motion. The increased motion causes the molecules to bounce off one another and move farther apart. The opposite occurs when the molecules of a gas cool down. The graph shows how the volume of a gas changes as its temperature changes.

Temperature and Volume of a Gas

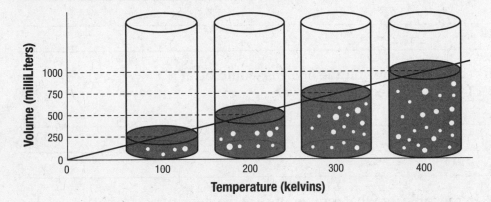

Most substances increase in volume when heated, including liquids, although liquids increase much less than gases. As the volume of a substance increases, its density decreases, because density is the ratio of mass to volume. The table shows how the density of liquid water changes as its temperature changes.

Temperature and Density of Water	
Temperature (°C)	Density (g/mL)
17	0.9988
18	0.9986
19	0.9984
20	0.9982
21	0.9980
22	0.9978
23	0.9976
24	0.9973
25	0.9971
26	0.9968
27	0.9965
28	0.9962
29	0.9959
30	0.9956
31	0.9953

Questions

1. **a. Identifying** In the graph, find the volume of a gas at a temperature of 100 K and at a temperature of 200 K. Record the temperatures and volumes.

_____

_____

b. Calculating By what factor does the volume of a gas increase when its temperature is doubled?

_____

_____

_____

c. Predicting Predict what the volume of a gas would be at a temperature of 600 K. Explain your answer.

_____

_____

_____

2. **a. Identifying** In the table, at what temperature is the density of water lowest? Highest? What is the density of water at those temperatures?

_____

_____

b. Calculating Calculate the average change in the density of water for each one-degree change in temperature.

_____

_____

_____

c. Inferring For each one-degree change in temperature, the change in volume and density of water is much less than the change in volume and density of mercury. Based on this fact, explain why water is not as suitable a liquid for a thermometer as mercury.

_____

_____

_____

_____

Chapter 3   States of Matter

Section 3.2   The Gas Laws
(pages 75–83)

Math ▶ Skills   *The Combined Gas Law*

Content and Vocabulary Support

Charles's Law

Charles's law describes how the volume of a gas is affected by a change in temperature. The law states that the volume of a gas is directly proportional to its temperature if its pressure and number of particles remain constant. Charles's law can be written as:

$$\frac{V_1}{T_1} = \frac{V_2}{T_2}$$

V_1 and T_1 represent the volume and temperature of the gas before a change in temperature occurs. V_2 and T_2 represent the volume and temperature of the gas after the temperature changes. Temperatures must be expressed in degrees Kelvin (K) for the formula to apply.

Boyle's Law

Boyle's law describes how the volume of a gas is affected by a change in pressure. The law states that the volume of a gas is inversely proportional to its pressure if its temperature and number of particles remain constant. Boyle's law can be written as:

$$P_1V_1 = P_2V_2$$

P_1 and V_1 are the pressure and volume of the gas before a change in pressure occurs. P_2 and V_2 are the pressure and volume of the gas after the pressure changes. Pressure is usually measured in kilopascals (kPa), and kPa = 0.0102 kg/cm^2.

The Combined Gas Law

Charles's law and Boyle's law can be combined into a single law called the combined gas law. The combined gas law describes the relationship among temperature, volume, and pressure of a gas when the number of particles is constant. The combined gas law can be written as:

$$\frac{P_1V_1}{T_1} = \frac{P_2V_2}{T_2}$$

Section 3.2 The Gas Laws

Solved Examples

Example 1: A 0.50-L container of air has a pressure of 200 kPa. If the pressure increases to 250 kPa, while the temperature remains the same, what is the new volume of air?

Given: $V_1 = 0.50$ L $P_1 = 200$ kPa $P_2 = 250$ kPa $T_1 = T_2$

Unknown: V_2 *Equation:* $\dfrac{P_1 V_1}{T_1} = \dfrac{P_2 V_2}{T_2}$

Solution: Solving the equation for V_2 gives:

$$V_2 = \frac{P_1 V_1 T_2}{T_1 P_2}$$

Because T_1 and T_2 are equal, they cancel each other out, leaving:

$$V_2 = \frac{P_1 V_1}{P_2}$$

Substituting the given values into this equation yields:

$$V_2 = \frac{(200 \text{ kPa}) \times (0.50\text{L})}{(250 \text{ kPa})} = 0.4 \text{ L}$$

Example 2: At a temperature of 200 K, a closed cylinder contains gas at a pressure of 400 kPa. If the temperature increases to 280 K, what is the new pressure?

Given: $T_1 = 200$ K $P_1 = 400$ kPa $T_2 = 280$ K $V_1 = V_2$

Unknown: P_2 *Equation:* $\dfrac{P_1 V_1}{T_1} = \dfrac{P_2 V_2}{T_2}$

Solution: Solving the equation for P_2 gives:

$$P_2 = \frac{P_1 V_1 T_2}{T_1 V_2}$$

Because V_1 and V_2 are equal, they cancel each other out, leaving:

$$P_2 = \frac{P_1 V_1 T_2}{T_1 V_2}$$

Substituting the given values into this equation yields:

$$P_2 = \frac{(400 \text{ kPa}) \times (280 \text{ K})}{(200 \text{ K})} = 560 \text{ kPa}$$

Practice Exercises

Exercise 1: At a given temperature, gas with a pressure of 150 kPa has a volume of 0.8 L. If the pressure decreases to 75 kPa and the temperature remains the same, what will be the volume of the gas?

Exercise 2: A liter of gas has a pressure of 200 kPa. If the gas is put into 2-L container, what will be its pressure, assuming its temperature does not change?

Exercise 3: A given volume of gas at a temperature of 100 K has a pressure of 225 kPa. At a higher temperature, the same volume of gas has a pressure of 450 kPa. At what temperature does the gas have this higher pressure?

Exercise 4: Gas under 200 kPa of pressure at a temperature of 120 K fills a 0.5-L container. If the temperature decreases to 80 K but the pressure stays the same, what volume will the gas have?

Exercise 5: A volume of 1.5 L liters of a gas at a temperature of 150 K has a pressure of 340 kPa. If the temperature of the gas increases to 200 K and the volume decreases to 1 L, what is the new pressure of the gas?

Chapter 6   Chemical Bonds

Section 6.1 Ionic Bonding
(pages 158–164)

 **Determining the Size and Mass of Atoms and Ions**

Content and Vocabulary Support

Electron Configuration

The configuration of the electrons in an atom refers to the number of electrons at different energy levels. It includes the number of valence electrons, which are electrons at the highest energy level. Atoms of different elements may have different numbers of valance electrons. For example, atoms of potassium (K) have one valence electron, and atoms of fluorine (F) have seven valence electrons. Valence electrons are represented by dots in an **electron dot diagram**, such as the one shown here for potassium.

$$K \cdot$$

Atoms of elements that do not have a complete set of valence electrons are somewhat unstable. They tend to react with other elements and become more stable. Some elements become more stable by transferring electrons between atoms. The diagram shows the transfer of electrons between potassium and fluorine.

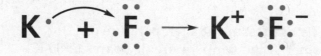

Ions

Electrons have a negative charge. Thus, when an atom gains electrons, it also becomes negative in charge. Similarly, when an atom loses electrons, it becomes positive in charge. An atom that has a negative or positive charge is called an **ion**. If the charge is negative, the ion is called an **anion**. If the charge is positive, the ion is called a **cation**. A cation is given the same name as the element name. For example, a potassium cation is called *potassium*. An anion is given a name based on the element name but with the suffix *-ide* added. The fluorine anion, for example, is called *fluoride*.

Size of Atoms and Ions

Scientists consider atoms and ions to be more or less spherical in shape. They use the radius of an atom or ion as a measure of its size. The radius is the distance from the center to the outer edge. It is such a tiny distance that it is expressed in a unit called a *picometer* (pm), which is just one-billionth of a millimeter.

Name _____ Class _____ Date _____

Section 6.1 Ionic Bonding

Data

Table 1 is part of a periodic table of the elements. For each element, the table shows atomic number (top), symbol (middle), and electron configuration (bottom).

Table 1. Electron Configurations of Atoms

Radii of Atoms and Ions			
1A	2A	6A	7A
11 **Na** 2-8-1	12 **Mg** 2-8-2	16 **S** 2-8-6	17 **Cl** 2-8-7
19 **K** 2-8-8-1	20 **Ca** 2-8-8-2	34 **Se** 2-8-18-6	35 **Br** 2-8-18-7
37 **Rb** 2-8-18-8-1	38 **Sr** 2-8-18-8-2	52 **Te** 2-8-18-18-6	53 **I** 2-8-18-18-7
55 **Cs** 2-8-18-18-8-1	56 **Ba** 2-8-18-18-8-2	84 **Po** 2-8-18-32-18-6	85 **At** 2-8-18-32-18-7

Table 2 is part of another periodic table. In addition to the symbol for each element, this table shows the radius of an atom (upper right), the radius of an ion of that atom (lower right), and the number of electrons the atom gains or loses in becoming the ion (lower left).

Table 2. Radii of Atoms and Ions

Radii of Atoms and Ions			
1A	2A	6A	7A
Li 152 / 1+ / 60	**Be** 112 / 2+ / 31	**O** 66 / 2− / 140	**F** 64 / 1− / 136
Na 186 / 1+ / 95	**Mg** 160 / 2+ / 65	**S** 103 / 2− / 184	**Cl** 99 / 1− / 181
K 227 / 1+ / 133	**Ca** 197 / 2+ / 99	**Se** 117 / 2− / 198	**Br** 114 / 1− / 195

Questions

1. **a. Describing** Based on Table 1, how do the electron configurations of atoms within each group change as you go from lower to higher atomic number? How do the electron configurations change as you go across the table from one group to another within a row?

_____

_____

_____

  b. Identifying Identify the number of valence electrons that characterize each of the four different Groups shown in Table 1.

_____

_____

  c. Predicting In order to become more stable, predict whether atoms of elements in Groups 1A and 2A in Table 1 would gain or lose electrons. Make a similar prediction about the atoms of elements in Groups 6A and 7A in Table 1.

_____

_____

_____

2. **a. Comparing and Contrasting** Check your predictions from question 1c by looking at Table 2 and finding the number of valence electrons gained or lost by atoms when they become ions. Compare Groups 1A and 2A with Groups 6A and 7A. For example, how many electrons are gained or lost by lithium (Li)? By oxygen (O)?

_____

_____

  b. Drawing Conclusions In general, how does an atom's radius change when it becomes a cation? An anion?

_____

_____

_____

  c. Predicting The last element in Group 1A is francium (Fr). It is not shown in either table. Predict how many valence electrons francium has, whether it gains or loses electrons to become an ion, and how its radius changes when it becomes an ion.

_____

_____

Chapter 6   Chemical Bonds

Section 6.3 Naming Compounds and Writing Formulas

(pages 170–175)

Math Skills *Writing Formulas for Ionic Compounds*

Content and Vocabulary Support

Names of Ionic Compounds

Names of ionic compounds are based on their composition. For example, a compound composed of calcium ions and oxide ions is called calcium oxide. A compound that consists of just two elements, such as calcium oxide, is called a binary compound. The name of a binary compound follows a simple rule: the name of the cation (positive ion) comes first, followed by the name of the anion (negative ion).

Some metals form more than type of ion. For example, iron forms an ion with a charge of positive two and an ion with a charge of positive three. Both iron ions can form compounds with the same anion, such as oxide. To tell these ions and their compounds apart, Roman numerals are used to distinguish the ions: iron (II) and iron (III).

A **polyatomic ion** is another type of ionic compound. It forms when a group of atoms bond covalently but act as a unit and have an overall positive or negative charge. An example of a polyatomic ion is sulfate. It consists of one sulfur atom and four oxygen atoms.

Writing Formulas for Ionic Compounds

Formulas for ionic compounds are a shorthand way of showing their composition. For example, the formula for calcium oxide is written CaO. The formula shows there is a one-to-one ratio of calcium ions (Ca^{2+}) to oxide ions (O^{2-}) in the compound. (The superscripts indicate the charge of the ions.)

In ionic compounds, the overall compound has no charge. In CaO, for example, the positive two charge of the calcium ions is balanced by the negative two charge of the oxygen ions. In sodium sulfide (Na_2S), on the other, the sodium ion (Na^+) has a charge of positive one, while the sulfide ion (S^{2-}) has a charge of negative two. Therefore, two sodium atoms are needed for each sulfide ion in sodium sulfide. This is indicated by the subscript 2 following Na in the formula, Na_2S. In sum, if you know the charges of the ions in an ionic compound, you can determine the correct ratio of ions and the subscripts to use in the formula.

Unlike other ionic compounds, polyatomic ions have a charge. This is written as a superscript, as it is for ions such as Ca^{2+}. For example, the polyatomic ion sulfate has one sulfur and four oxygen atoms and a charge of negative two. Its formula is SO_4^{2-}.

Section 6.3 Naming Compounds and Writing Formulas

Solved Examples

Example 1: Write the formula for sodium chloride.

Given: Name of compound = sodium (Na) chloride (Cl)

Unknown: Charges of sodium ions and chloride ions ratio of sodium ions to chloride ions in compound

Solution: From the table of anions on page 171 of the textbook, chloride has a charge of negative one. The positive charge of a metal is usually the same as its group number in the periodic table. Sodium is in group one, so it has a charge of positive one. Based on the ion charges, there must be a one-to-one ratio between sodium and chloride in the compound. Therefore, the formula for sodium chloride is NaCl.

Example 2: The symbol for iron is Fe. Write the formula for iron (II) oxide.

Given: Name of compound = iron (II) oxide

Unknown: Charges of iron (II) ions and oxide ions ratio of iron (II) ions to oxide ions in compound

Solution: From the "(II)" in its name, you know that the charge of the iron (II) ion is positive two. From the table of anions on page 171, oxide has a charge of negative two. Therefore, the ratio of iron (II) to oxide ions must be one-to-one, and the formula is FeO.

Example 3: Write the formula for the polyatomic ion silicate. It consists of silicon (Si) and oxygen in a one-to-three ratio and has an overall charge of negative two.

Given: Ratio of silicon to oxygen atoms in compound = 1:3 charge of compound − 2−

Unknown: Formula for compound

Solution: Based on the information given, the formula for silicate is: SiO_3^{2-}.

Practice Exercises

Exercise 1: The formula for an ionic compound is $CaBr_2$. What is the name of the compound?

Exercise 2: What are the formulas for the ionic compounds named sodium iodide and magnesium iodide?

Exercise 3: Write the formula for iron (III) phosphide.

Exercise 4: The symbol for the metal chromium is Cr. What is the formula for chromium (II) sulfide?

Exercise 5: Chromate is a polyatomic ion with a charge of negative two. It contains chromium and oxygen in a one-to-four ratio. What is its formula?

Chapter 7   Chemical Reactions

Section 7.1 Describing Reactions
(pages 192–198)

Math **Skills** *Balancing Chemical Equations*

Content and Vocabulary Support

Chemical Equations

In a chemical reaction, the substances that undergo change are called **reactants**. The new substances that are formed are called **products**. A **chemical equation** is a way of representing a chemical reaction in which the reactants and products are expressed as formulas. For example, carbon reacts with oxygen to form carbon monoxide. The chemical equation for this reaction is:

$$C + O \rightarrow CO$$

The number of each type of atom is always the same on both sides of the equation. This is due to the law of conservation of mass, which states that mass is neither created nor destroyed in a chemical reaction.

Balancing Chemical Equations

In order for some chemical equations to be balanced, there must be more of some reactants or products than others. For example, iron (Fe) reacts with oxide (O_2) to produce iron oxide (FeO). However, just writing:

$$Fe + O_2 \rightarrow FeO$$

leads to a chemical equation that is not balanced. The left side has twice as many oxygen atoms as the right side. The first step in balancing this equation is to double the number of oxygen atoms on the right side by writing the number "2" in front of the FeO:

$$Fe + O_2 \rightarrow 2\ FeO$$

This number is called a **coefficient**. Coefficients in a chemical equation give the ratios of reactants and products in the reaction. When there is no coefficient given, it is assumed to be 1. To finish balancing the equation, Fe also must be given a coefficient of 2:

$$2\ Fe + O_2 \rightarrow 2\ FeO$$

Section 7.1 Describing Reactions

Solved Examples

Example 1: Nitrogen (N_2) reacts with oxygen (O_2) to produce dinitrogen tetroxide (N_2O_4), a component of rocket fuel. Write and balance the chemical equation for this reaction.

Given: Reactants = N_2, O_2
Product = N_2O_4

Unknown: Equation

Solution: Add the reactants on the left, and link them with an arrow to the product on the right:

$$N_2 + O_2 \times N_2O_4$$

Change the coefficient of O_2 to balance the number of oxygen atoms:

$$N_2 + 2\,O_2 \times N_2O_4$$

Example 2: In the burning of natural gas, methane (CH_4) reacts with oxygen (O_2) to form carbon dioxide (CO_2) and water (H_2O). Write and balance the chemical equation for this reaction.

Given: Reactants = CH_4, O_2
Products = CO_2, H_2O

Unknown: Equation

Solution: Place the reactants on the left and the products on the right:

$$CH_4 + O_2 \times CO_2 + H_2O$$

Balance the number of oxygen and hydrogen atoms by changing the coefficients of O_2 and H_2O:

$$CH_4 + 2\,O_2 \times CO_2 + 2\,H_2O$$

Name _____ Class _____ Date _____

Practice Exercises

Exercise 1: Hydrogen (H_2) and oxygen (O_2) react to form water
(H_2O). Write and balance the equation for this reaction.

Exercise 2: Determine if the following equation is balanced, and
then balance it if needed.

$$CaO + HCL \rightarrow CaCl_2 + H_2O$$

Exercise 3: Write and balance an equation for a reaction in which
iron (Fe) and hydrochloric acid (HCL) react to form iron
chloride ($FeCl_2$) and hydrogen (H_2).

Exercise 4: Dissolving sodium (Na) in water produces sodium
oxide (NaOH) and hydrogen (H_2). Write a balanced
equation for this reaction.

Exercise 5: If you add heat to potassium chlorate ($KClO_3$), it reacts
and forms potassium chloride (KCl) and oxygen (O_2).
Write and balance the equation for this reaction.

Chapter 8   Solutions, Acids, and Bases

Section 8.2 Solubility and Concentration
(pages 235–239)

Math Skills *Calculating the Concentration of Solutions*

Content and Vocabulary Support

Concentration of Solutions

The **concentration** of a solution is the amount of solute dissolved in a specified amount of solution. Concentration can be expressed in three different ways: percent by volume, percent by mass, and molarity.

Percent by Volume

The percent by volume of a solute in a solution can be calculated using the equation:

$$\text{Percent by volume} = \frac{\text{Volume of solute}}{\text{Volume of solution}} \times 100\%$$

This measure of concentration is a good choice when the solute is a liquid, such as fruit juice, dissolved in water.

Percent by Mass

The percent by mass of a solute in a solution can be calculated using the equation:

$$\text{Percent by mass} = \frac{\text{Mass of solute}}{\text{Mass of solution}} \times 100\%$$

This measure of concentration is a good choice when the solute is a solid, such as salt, dissolved in water.

Molarity

Molarity is the number of moles of a solute per liter of solution. The molarity of a solution can be calculated using the equation:

$$\text{Molarity} = \frac{\text{Moles of solute}}{\text{Moles of solution}}$$

The grams in one mole of a substance are equal to its mass number. The mass number of elements can be found in the periodic table. For example, water (H_2O) has a mass number of 18, because each hydrogen atom has a mass number of 1 and oxygen has a mass number of 16. Thus, one mole of water has a mass of 18 g.

Section 8.2 Solubility and Concentration

Solved Examples

Example 1: In science lab, Ty makes a solution of 10 mL of acid and 200 mL of water. What is the concentration of acid in the solution?

Given: Volume of solute = 10 mL
Volume of solution = 200 mL

Unknown: Concentration

Equation: Percent by volume = $\dfrac{\text{Volume of solute}}{\text{Volume of solution}} \times 100\%$

Solution: Percent by volume = $\dfrac{10\text{mL}}{200\text{mL}} \times 100\% = 5\%$

Example 2: A 500-mL bottle of fruit drink has a concentration of 22% juice. What is the volume of juice in the drink?

Given: Volume of solution = 500 mL
Percent by volume = 22%

Unknown: Volume of solute

Equation: Percent by volume = $\dfrac{\text{Volume of solute}}{\text{Volume of solution}} \times 100\%$

Solution: Solving the equation for "volume of solute" gives:

Volume of solute = $\dfrac{\text{percent by volume} \times \text{volume of solution}}{100\%}$

Substituting the given values in this equation yields:

Volume of solute = $\dfrac{22\% \times 500 \text{ ml}}{100\%} = 110 \text{ mL}$

Example 3: A 30-kg sample of water has 1.2 g of dissolved minerals. What is the concentration of minerals in the water?

Given: Mass of solution = 30 kg, or 30,000 g
Mass of solute = 1.2 g

Unknown: Concentration

Equation: Percent by mass = $\dfrac{\text{Moles of solute}}{\text{Moles of solution}} \times 100\%$

Solution: Percent by mass = $\dfrac{1.2 \text{ g}}{30,000 \text{ g}} \times 100\% = 0.004\%$

Example 4: One mole of sodium chloride (NaCl) is 58 g. If 116 g of sodium chloride are added to 3 L of water, what is the molarity?

Given: Grams of solute = 116 g
Liters of water = 3 L

Unknown: Moles of solute
Molarity

Equation: Molarity = $\dfrac{\text{Moles of solute}}{\text{Moles of solution}}$

Solution: One mole of sodium chloride is 58 g, so 116 g of sodium chloride is 2 moles. Substituting in the equation gives:

$$\text{Molarity} = \frac{2 \text{ moles}}{3 \text{L}} = 0.67$$

Example 5: Jorge wants to add ammonia (NH_3) to 2 L liters of water to make a solution with molarity of 1.0. How many grams of ammonia does he need?

Given: Liters of solution = 2 L
Molarity = 1.0

Unknowns: Moles of solute
Grams of solute

Equation: Molarity = $\dfrac{\text{moles of solute}}{\text{liters of solution}}$

Solution: Solving the equation for "moles of solute" gives:

Moles of solute = molarity × liters of solution

Substituting the given values yields:

Moles of solute = 1.0 × 2 L = 2 moles

The mass number of ammonia is 17 (14 for nitrogen plus 1 for each of the three hydrogen atoms). Therefore, 1 mole of ammonia is 17 g, and 2 moles of ammonia are 34 g.

Practice Exercises

Exercise 1: Find the volume of a liquid solute in a 500-mL solution in which the solute has a concentration of 2.4%.

Exercise 2: An all-purpose disinfectant can be made by adding 50 mL of liquid bleach to 500 mL of tap water. What is the concentration of bleach in the resulting solution?

Exercise 3: Kara is dissolving lemon juice in water to make a liter of lemonade. She wants the resulting solution to have a 25 percent concentration of lemon juice by volume. How much lemon juice should she use?

Exercise 4: Tito made a juice drink from a powdered concentrate. He added 10 g of powder to 2 kg of water. What is the concentration of powder in the drink?

Exercise 5: A chemistry teacher has only 12 g of a solute that she needs to make a 15%-concentration solution in distilled water. How many grams of solution at this concentration can she make with 12 g of solute?

Exercise 6: Which salt water solution has a greater concentration: one in which 5 g of salt were used to make 330 g of solution, or one in which 8 mL of salt were used to make 400 mL of solution?

Exercise 7: One mole of a type of alcohol is 46 g. What is the molarity of a solution of 46 g of the alcohol dissolved in 2 L of water?

Exercise 8: How many moles of nitric acid (HNO_3) are needed to make 2 liters of a solution of nitric acid in water with a molarity of 1?

Exercise 9: Find the number of grams in 1 mole of sulfuric acid (H_2SO_4). Then, calculate the number of grams of sulfuric acid needed to make a 1-L solution of sulfuric acid in water that has a molarity of 1.5.

Exercise 10: A 2-L solution of nitric acid (HNO_3) in water contains 126 g of nitric acid. A 1-L solution of phosphoric acid (H_3PO_4) contains 98 g of phosphoric acid. Which solution has greater molarity?

Chapter 9   Carbon Chemistry

Section 9.2 Substituted Hydrocarbons

(pages 272–274)

 *Analyzing Properties of Substituted Hydrocarbons*

Content and Vocabulary Support

Substituted Hydrocarbons

A hydrocarbon in which one or more hydrogen atoms have been replaced by another atom or group of atoms is called a **substituted hydrocarbon**. The substituted atom or group of atoms is called a **functional group**, because it determines the properties of the compound. Examples of substituted hydrocarbons include alcohols, organic acids and bases, and esters. Each of these types of substituted hydrocarbons has a different functional group and therefore different properties.

Alcohols

The functional group in alcohols is a hydroxyl group, $-OH$. The names of alcohols end in *–ol*. Examples of alcohols include methanol (CH_3OH), which is the simplest alcohol, and ethanol (C_2H_5OH), another simple alcohol.

Organic Acids and Bases

The functional group in organic acids is a carboxyl group, $-COOH$. Names of organic acids end in *–oic*. Examples are methanoic acid ($HCOOH$) and ethanoic acid (CH_3COOH).

The functional group in organic bases is an amino group, $-NH_2$. Organic bases are called amines. Examples are adenine and thymine. Both are components of DNA molecules.

Esters

Esters form when organic acids react with alcohols. Water is also produced in this type of reaction. For example, ethanoic acid reacts with methanol to produce an ester called *methyl acetate* and water.

Properties of Substituted Hydrocarbons

Each type of substituted hydrocarbon has its own particular characteristics. For example, organic acids taste sour, and esters have pleasant odors and flavors. Within each type of substituted hydrocarbons, there is also variation in the properties of the different compounds.

Section 9.2 Substituted Hydrocarbons

Data

Table 1 shows the boiling points of several different alcohols. Each type of alcohol is formed by substituting a carboxyl group (–OH) for hydrogen (H) in a straight-chain alkane. Methanol is formed by substituting –OH for H in methane (CH_4), ethanol by substituting –OH for H in ethane (C_2H_6), and so on.

Table 1. Boiling Points of Alcohols		
Name	*Formula*	*Boiling Point (°C)*
Methanol	CH_3OH	65
Ethanol	C_2H_5OH	79
Propanol	C_3H_7OH	97
Butanol	C_4H_9OH	118

Table 2 shows the boiling points of several different chlorocarbons. Each type of chlorocarbon is formed by substituting one or more chlorine (Cl) atoms for hydrogen in a single methane molecule.

Table 2. Boiling Points of Chlorocarbons		
Name	*Formula*	*Boiling Point (°C)*
Chloromethane	CH_3Cl	−24
Dichloromethane	CH_2Cl_2	40
Trichloromethane	$CHCl_3$	61
Tetrachloromethane	CCl_4	77

Questions

1. **a. Observing** In Table 1, how many substitutions of –OH for H are made each time an alcohol is formed?

   _____

   _____

   b. Comparing and Contrasting How do the alcohols in Table 1 differ from one another?

   _____

   _____

   _____

   c. Inferring What is the relationship between the size of alcohol molecules and their boiling points?

   _____

   _____

   _____

2. **a. Describing** Describe how the number of substitutions of Cl for H changes from the top to the bottom of Table 2.

   _____

   _____

   _____

   b. Calculating Find the mass numbers of carbon, chlorine, and hydrogen in the periodic table. Then, calculate the mass numbers of chloromethane and tetrachloromethane.

   _____

   _____

   _____

   c. Inferring What is the relationship between the mass number of chlorocarbons and their boiling point?

   _____

   _____

   _____

Chapter 10   Nuclear Chemistry

Section 10.1 Radioactivity
(pages 292–297)

Math Skills *Balancing Nuclear Equations*

Content and Vocabulary Support

Nuclear Decay

Radioactivity is the process in which an unstable atomic nucleus gives off charged particles and energy. Atoms with an unstable nucleus are called radioactive isotopes, or **radioisotopes**. As radioisotopes give off charged particles, they gradually change into other isotopes or elements. This process is called **nuclear decay**. For example, uranium-238 undergoes nuclear decay and changes into thorium-234. (The numbers are the mass numbers of the isotopes.)

Nuclear Radiation

The charged particles and energy given off by radioisotopes are called **nuclear radiation.** Common types of nuclear radiation are alpha particles, beta particles, and gamma rays.

The release of alpha particles is called alpha decay. An **alpha particle** is a particle made up of two protons and two neutrons. It has a mass number of four and a charge of positive two. It is represented by the symbol $_2^4\text{He}$. The top number in the symbol (4) is the mass number, and the bottom number (2) is the atomic number.

The release of beta particles is called beta decay. A **beta particle** is an electron given off by a radioisotope. It has a mass number of zero and a charge of negative one. It is represented by the symbol $_{-1}^{0}e$.

Gamma rays are rays of energy given off by a radioisotope. Gamma rays have no mass and no charge. They are represented by the symbol γ.

Nuclear Equations

Radioactive decay reactions are represented by nuclear equations. For example, when uranium-238 decays to thorium-234, it gives off alpha particles. The nuclear equation for this reaction is:

$$_{92}^{238}\text{U} \rightarrow \, _{90}^{234}\text{Th} + \, _2^4\text{He}$$

Like equations for other types of reactions, nuclear equations must balance. To be balanced, total mass numbers and atomic numbers must be the same on both sides of the equation.

Section 10.1 Radioactivity

Solved Examples

Example 1: Write a balanced nuclear equation for the beta decay of thorium-234.

Given: Reactant radioisotope: thorium-234

Type of nuclear radiation: $_{-1}^{0}e$

Unknown: Product radioisotope (X)

Solution: From the periodic table, the atomic number of thorium is 90. Place thorium on the left side of the equation with its mass number and atomic number. On the right side, place X plus the beta particle:

$$_{90}^{234}\text{Th} \rightarrow X + _{-1}^{0}e$$

The atomic mass and atomic number of X must balance the equation. Therefore, the atomic mass of X must be 234 (234 = <u>234</u> + 0), and the atomic number of X must be 91 (90 = <u>91</u>-1). From the periodic table, the element with an atomic number of 91 is protactinium (Pa). The final balanced equation is:

$$_{90}^{234}\text{Th} \rightarrow _{91}^{234}\text{Pa} + _{-1}^{0}e$$

Example 2: When radon-222 undergoes alpha decay, what is the product radioisotope?

Given: Reactant radioisotope: radon-222

Type of nuclear radiation: $_{2}^{4}\text{He}$

Unknown: Product radioisotope (X)

Solution: From the periodic table, the atomic number of radon is 86. Place radon on the left side of the equation. Place X and the alpha particle on the right:

$$_{86}^{222}\text{Rn} \rightarrow X + _{2}^{4}\text{He}$$

The atomic mass of X must be 218 (222 = <u>218</u> + 4), and the atomic number must be 84 (86 = <u>84</u> +2). From the periodic table, the element with atomic number of 84 is polonium (Po). Therefore, the equation is:

$$_{86}^{222}\text{Rn} \rightarrow _{84}^{218}\text{Po} + _{2}^{4}\text{He}$$

Name _____ Class _____ Date _____

Practice Exercises

Exercise 1: When Polonium-218 undergoes alpha decay, it produces lead (Pb). Write a balanced equation for this reaction.

Exercise 2: Write a balanced equation for the beta decay of protactinium-234.

Exercise 3: What is the product radioisotope of the alpha decay of uranium-234?

Exercise 4: What radioactive isotope undergoes alpha decay to produce radium-226?

Exercise 5: What type of radioactive decay occurs when lead-210 becomes bismuth-210?

Chapter 11   Motion

Section 11.2 Speed and Velocity
(pages 332–337)

Math Skills *Calculating Average Speed*

Content and Vocabulary Support

Speed

Speed is a measure of how fast something is moving. It is calculated by dividing the distance an object moves by the amount of time it takes the object to move that distance. For example, a car that travels 50 kilometers in one hour has a speed of 50 km/h. In other words, speed is a ratio of distance to time.

Many objects do not move at a constant speed. For example, a car traveling at a speed of 50 km/h may slow down as it approaches a red light and then speed up again when the light turns green. The car's speed at any given moment in time is called its **instantaneous speed**.

Average Speed

Although an object may not have a constant speed, its motion over a given distance can be expressed as its average speed. **Average speed** is the total distance traveled, divided by the total time it takes to travel that distance. The equation for average speed is:

$$\text{Average speed} = \frac{\text{Total distance}}{\text{Total time}}, \text{ or } \overline{v} = \frac{d}{t}$$

For example, if a car travels 80 kilometers in the first hour of a two-hour trip and 100 kilometers in the second hour, its average speed for the total trip would be:

$$\overline{v} = \frac{(80 \text{ km} + 100 \text{ km})}{(1 \text{ h} + 1 \text{ h})} = \frac{180 \text{ km}}{2 \text{ h}} = 90 \text{ km/hr}$$

The equation for average speed can be rewritten to find either the total time or the total distance when the other two variables are known:

$$t = \frac{d}{\overline{v}} \text{ and } d = \overline{v} \times t$$

Section 11.2 Speed and Velocity

Solved Examples

Example 1: A winner of the Indianapolis 500 auto race completed the 806.5-kilometer race in 2.98 hours. What was the driver's average speed during the race?

Given: Total distance (d) = 806.5 km
Total time (t) = 2.98 h

Unknown: Average speed ($\bar{v}$)

Equation: $\bar{v} = \dfrac{d}{t}$

Solution: $\bar{v} = \dfrac{806.5 \text{ km}}{2.98 \text{ h}} = 270.6 \text{ km/h}$

Example 2: Different animal species show a tremendous range of variation in their speed of movement. The fastest land animal, the cheetah, can travel 100.0 km/h. In contrast, the slowest animal, a species of sea crab, has an average speed of just 5.7 km/y. How long would it take the sea crab to travel 100.0 km?

Given: Average speed ($\bar{v}$) = 5.7 km/y
Total distance (d) = 100 km

Unknown: Total time (t)

Equation: $t = \dfrac{d}{\bar{v}}$

Solution: $t = \dfrac{100 \text{ km}}{5.7 \text{ km/y}} = 17.5 \text{ y}$

Example 3: You usually see lightning before you hear thunder, because light travels faster than sound. Juan saw a flash of lightning and heard the thunder 6 seconds later. Sound travels at a speed of 340 m/s in air. How far away was Juan from the lightning?

Given: Average speed ($\bar{v}$) = 340m/s
Total time (t) = 6 s

Unknown: Total distance (d)

Equation: $d = \bar{v} \times t$

Solution: $d = (340 \text{ m/s}) \times (6 \text{ s}) = 2{,}040 \text{ m}$

Name _____   Class _____   Date _____

Practice Exercises

Exercise 1:   In a boat race, Dan drove his motorboat over the 1000-meter course from start to finish in 40 seconds. What was Dan's average speed during the race?

Exercise 2:   It takes Serina 0.25 hour to drive to school. Her route is 16 km long. What is Serina's average speed on her drive to school?

Exercise 3:   In a competition, an athlete threw a flying disk 139 meters through the air. While in flight, the disk traveled at an average speed of 13.0 m/s. How long did the disk remain in flight?

Exercise 4:   If you shout into Grand Canyon, your voice travels at the speed of sound (340 m/s) to the bottom of the canyon and back, and you hear an echo. How deep is the Grand Canyon in a spot where you can hear your echo 5.2 seconds after you shout?

Exercise 5:   Sound travels much faster in water than air. It takes 4.2 seconds for the sound of an explosion to travel underwater to a diver 6,006 m away. What is the speed of sound in water?

Chapter 11   Motion

Section 11.3 Acceleration
(pages 342–348)

Math Skills *Calculating Acceleration*

Content and Vocabulary Support

Acceleration

The rate at which velocity changes is called **acceleration**. Recall that velocity refers to both speed and direction. Therefore, acceleration also refers to changes in both speed and direction.

Acceleration as a change in speed is the most common use of the term. Recall that the unit for speed is meters per second (m/s). The unit for acceleration as a change in speed is meters per second per second, or meters per second squared (m/s^2).

An example of acceleration as a change in speed is free fall. **Free fall** is the movement of an object toward Earth solely because of gravity. The acceleration of an object in free fall is $9.8 \ m/s^2$. This means that each second the object falls toward Earth, its speed increases by $9.8 \ m/s^2$.

Acceleration as a change in speed can be negative as well as positive. For example, if a car slows down as it approaches a red light, its change in speed is negative. Therefore, the car's acceleration is negative. Negative acceleration is often called deceleration.

Acceleration can also occur as a change in direction. For example, if a car travels around a curve at a constant speed, it is still accelerating because of the change in the direction. If the car also slows down as it rounds the curve, it is accelerating in both speed and direction.

Constant acceleration refers to a steady change in velocity. The velocity of an object undergoing constant acceleration changes by the same amount each second. The acceleration of an object in free fall is an example of constant acceleration.

Calculating Acceleration

Acceleration as a change in velocity for straight-line motion is calculated using the formula:

$$\text{Acceleration } (a) = \frac{\text{Change in velocity}}{\text{Total time}} = \frac{\overline{v}_f - \overline{v}_i}{t}$$

The variable $\overline{v}_f$ is the final velocity; $\overline{v}_i$ is the initial, or beginning, velocity; and t is the total time. The formula assumes that acceleration (a) is constant.

Section 11.3 Acceleration

Solved Examples

Example 1: Sami coasted on her bike straight down a hill, accelerating from a speed of 3 m/s to 9 m/s in a total time of 6 s. What was her acceleration?

Given: $\overline{v}_f = 9$ m/s $\overline{v}_i = 3$ m/s $t = 6$ s

Unknown: a   *Equation:* $a = \dfrac{\overline{v}_f - \overline{v}_i}{t}$

Solution: Substituting the given values into the equation yields:

$$a = \frac{(9 \text{ m/s} - 3 \text{ m/s}^2)}{6 \text{ s}} = 1 \text{ m/s}^2$$

Example 2: A train travels at a constant acceleration of 6 m/s², starting from a standstill at a station and traveling along a straight track. How long does it take the train to reach 72 m/s?

Given: $\overline{v}_f = 72$ m/s $\overline{v}_i = 0$ m/s $a = 6$ m/s²

Unknown: t   *Equation:* $a = \dfrac{\overline{v}_f - \overline{v}_i}{t}$

Solution: Solving the equation for *t* gives:

$$t = \frac{\overline{v}_f - \overline{v}_i}{a}$$

Substituting the given values into this equation yields:

$$t = \frac{(72 \text{ m/s} - 0 \text{ m/s})}{6 \text{ m/s}^2} = 12 \text{ s}$$

Example 3: A ball is thrown straight up in the air and then falls back to Earth. If the downward fall takes 2.2 s, how fast is the ball traveling when it strikes the ground?

Given: $\overline{v}_i = 0$ m/s $a = 9.8$ m/s² $t = 2.2$ s

Unknown: $\overline{v}_f$ *Equation:* $a = \dfrac{\overline{v}_f - \overline{v}_i}{t}$

Solution: Solving the equation for $\overline{v}_f$ gives:

$$\overline{v}_f = (a \times t) + \overline{v}_i$$

Substituting the given values in this equation yields:

$$\overline{v}_f = (9.8 \text{ m/s}^2 \times 2.2 \text{ s}) + 0 \text{ m/s} = 21.6 \text{ m/s}$$

Practice Exercises

Exercise 1: A car traveling at 12 m/s slows down at a constant rate for 4 seconds until it stops. What is its acceleration?

Exercise 2: A runner covers the last straight stretch of a race in 4 s. During that time, he speeds up from 5 m/s to 9 m/s. What is the runner's acceleration in this part of the race?

Exercise 3: A pebble fell from a bridge to the water below. The pebble entered the water at a speed of 19.6 m/s. How long did it take the pebble to reach the water from the bridge?

Exercise 4: Josh rolled a bowling ball down a lane in 2.5 s. The ball traveled at a constant acceleration of 1.8 m/s^2 down the lane and was traveling at a speed of 7.6 m/s by the time it reached the pins at the end of the lane. How fast was the ball going when it left Tim's hand?

Exercise 5: How long does it take a jet to accelerate from 200 m/s to 300 m/s with a constant acceleration of 50 m/s?

Chapter 12   Forces and Motion

Section 12.2 Newton's First and Second Laws of Motion

(pages 363–371)

Math Skills *Using Newton's Second Law*

Content and Vocabulary Support

Newton's First Law of Motion

Newton's first law of motion states that the motion of an object does not change as long as the net force acting on the object is zero. In other words, an object at rest tends to remain at rest, and an object in motion tends to remain in motion. For example, a soccer ball lying on the ground does not move until a force, such as a kick, causes it to move. Once in motion, it will continue to move until another force, such as friction or a wall, causes it to slow down or stop. Newton's first law is also called the law of inertia. **Inertia** is the tendency of an object to resist a change in its motion.

Newton's Second Law of Motion

Objects change their motion, or accelerate, when unbalanced forces are applied to them. For example, if a rolling soccer ball starts to roll up a slope, it will decrease in velocity until it stops. Then, it will roll back down the slope at an increasing velocity. Two forces—inertia and gravity—are acting on the ball. They are acting together when the ball is rolling down the slope and against each other when the ball is rolling up the slope. Their combined force on the ball is the net force.

Newton's second law of motion states that the acceleration of an object is equal to the net force acting on it divided by the object's mass. **Mass** is a measure of the inertia of an object and depends on the amount of matter the object contains. Newton's second law can be expressed by the equation:

$$\text{Acceleration} = \frac{\text{Net force}}{\text{Mass}}, \text{ or } a = \frac{F}{m}$$

An object with less mass or greater net force has greater acceleration.

Weight

Weight is the force of gravity acting on an object. The equation for weight is:

$$\text{Weight} = \text{Mass} \times \text{Acceleration due to gravity, or } W = mg$$

Acceleration due to gravity (g) is 9.8 m/s^2.

Section 12.2 Newton's First and Second Laws of Motion

Solved Examples

Example 1:   Erin threw a 3.0-kilogram ball with a net force of 210 newtons. What was the ball's acceleration?

Given: Net force (F) = 210 N
Mass (m) = 3.0 kg

Unknown: Acceleration (a)

Equation: $a = \dfrac{F}{m}$

Solution: $a = \dfrac{210 \text{ N}}{3.0 \text{ kg}} = 70 \text{ N/kg}$

The answer, 70 N/kg, can also be expressed as 70 m/s^2, because the unit N/kg equals m/s^2.

Example 2:   A 1,200-kilogram car accelerates at 4.5 m/s^2. What is the net force of the car?

Given: Mass (m) = 1,200 kg
Acceleration (a) = 4.5 m/s^2 = 4.5 N/kg

Unknown: Net force (F)

Equation: $a = \dfrac{F}{m}$

Solution: Solve the equation for F, and substitute the given values:

$$F = a \times m; F = 4.5 \text{ N/kg} \times 1{,}200 \text{ kg} = 5{,}400 \text{ N}$$

Example 3:   Find the mass of a person whose weight is 490 N.

Given: Weight (W) = 490 N
Acceleration due to gravity (g) = 9.8 m/s^2 = 9.8 N/kg

Unknown: Mass (m)

Equation: $W = mg$

Solution: Solve the equation for m, and substitute the given values:

$$m = \dfrac{W}{g}; m = \dfrac{490 \text{ N}}{9.8 \text{ N/kg}} = 50 \text{ kg}$$

Practice Exercises

Exercise 1:   What is the acceleration of a 1,500-kilogram truck with
            a net force of 7,500 newtons?

Exercise 2:   A runner with a mass of 60 kilograms accelerates at
            2.2 m/s^2. What is the runner's net force?

Exercise 3:   Find the mass of a flying discus that has a net force of
            1.05 newtons and accelerates at 3.5 m/s^2.

Exercise 4:   Ian has a mass of 58.0 kilograms. What is his weight?

Exercise 5:   Find the mass of a book that has a weight of
            14.7 newtons.

Chapter 12   Forces and Motion

Section 12.3 Newton's Third Law of Motion and Momentum

(pages 372–377)

Data **Analysis** *Analyzing Momentum*

Content and Vocabulary Support

Momentum

Momentum is the product of an object's mass and velocity. The larger the mass of an object or the faster it is moving, the larger its momentum. If an object has large momentum, it is hard to stop. Imagine trying to stop a car rolling very slowly down a slope. It would be hard to do because of the large mass of the car, not because of the car's velocity. It would also be hard to stop an object with a small mass but great velocity, such as a baseball traveling more than 100 kilometers per hour. The baseball's speed would give it large momentum.

Momentum Formula

The formula for calculating the momentum of an object is:

Momentum = Mass × Velocity

Momentum is measured in units of kilogram-meters per second, written kg·m/s. For example, the momentum of a golf ball with a mass of 0.05 kilograms and a speed of 58 meters per second is:

Momentum = 0.05 kg × 58 m/s = 2.9 kg·m/s

The equation for momentum can be rewritten to find mass or velocity if momentum is known:

$$\text{Mass} = \frac{\text{Momentum}}{\text{Velocity}}$$

$$\text{Velocity} = \frac{\text{Momentum}}{\text{Mass}}$$

Law of Conservation of Momentum

According to the **law of conservation of momentum**, within a system total momentum does not change. If one object loses momentum, another object gains momentum. Thus, momentum is conserved. For example, a baseball bat loses velocity and momentum when it hits a ball. However, the ball gains velocity and momentum when the bat strikes it.

Section 12.3 Newton's Third Law of Motion and Momentum

Data

A teacher is demonstrating the relationship between velocity and momentum. She drops a 0.03-kilogram object from the school roof to the lawn below. The graph shows the momentum of the object from the time it leaves the roof until it lands on the lawn.

Momentum of 0.03-kg Object in Free Fall

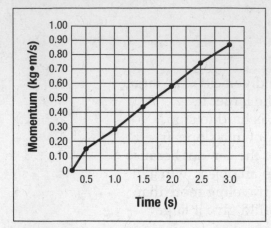

The table shows the momentum of several cars. Each has a different mass, but all are traveling at the same constant velocity.

Momentum of Cars with a Velocity of 20 m/s		
Car	Mass (kg)	Momentum (kg·m/s)
Car A	1,400	28,000
Car B	?	27,200
Car C	1,280	25,600
Car D	1,140	?
Car E	1,050	21,000

Name _____ Class _____ Date _____

Questions

1. a. **Describing** Based on the graph, describe how momentum changes with time for an object in free fall.

   _____

   _____

   _____

   b. **Calculating** Use the object's momentum and mass to calculate its velocity at 1.0 second and 3.0 seconds.

   _____

   _____

   _____

   c. **Relating Cause and Effect** What causes the momentum of the object to change as it falls?

   _____

   _____

   _____

2. a. **Identifying** Identify the car with the smallest momentum and the car with the largest momentum. What is the mass of each of these cars?

   _____

   _____

   _____

   b. **Calculating** Based on its momentum and velocity, calculate the mass of car B. Based on its mass and velocity, calculate the momentum of car D.

   _____

   _____

   _____

   _____

   c. **Controlling Variables** How could you increase the momentum of car E to equal the momentum of car A?

   _____

   _____

   _____

Chapter 13 Forces in Fluids

Section 13.1 Fluid Pressure
(pages 390–393)

Data **Analysis** *Analyzing Pressure*

Content and Vocabulary Support

Pressure

Pressure is the result of force distributed over an area. The equation for calculating pressure is:

$$\text{Pressure} = \frac{\text{Force}}{\text{Area}}$$

Force is measured in newtons (N), and area is measured in square meters (m^2). Pressure is measured in a unit called the **pascal** (Pa), which is the same as newtons per square meter (N/m^2). A kilopascal (kPa) is equal to 1,000 pascals. Recall that weight is also a unit of force, the force due to gravity, measured in newtons.

Consider the following example. A book lying on a table has a weight of 10 newtons, and its back cover has an area of 0.05 square meters. The pressure exerted by the book is:

$$\text{Pressure} = \frac{10N}{0.05 \ m^2} = 200 \ Pa$$

If the same amount of force is applied over a larger area, the amount of pressure exerted by the force is less. For example, a book with the same weight but a larger cover would exert less pressure. The reverse is also true: when the area is smaller, the pressure is greater.

Pressure in Fluids

A **fluid** is a substance that takes on the shape of its container. Fluids include both liquids and gases. The particles of a fluid exert pressure in all directions around them. For a fluid that is not moving, the amount of pressure the fluid exerts depends on two factors: type of fluid and depth of fluid. As the fluid's depth increases, the pressure of the fluid also increases. For example, at greater depths in a lake, water exerts more pressure on a diver.

Atmospheric Pressure

Air in Earth's atmosphere is a fluid. The weight of the atmosphere exerts a pressure of about 101 kPa at sea level. As distance above sea level (altitude) increases, depth of the atmosphere decreases. As a result, at higher altitudes, air pressure is lower than it is at sea level.

The pressure of the atmosphere is very great. However, it does not crush people and objects. This is because air, like other fluids, exerts pressure in all directions. The pressure on the outside of your body, for example, is balanced by the pressure on the inside of your body.

Section 13.1 Fluid Pressure

Data

Ted has five boxes with the same weight but different shapes. The boxes vary in the area of the bottom side. Table 1 shows the pressure of the boxes as they rest on a table.

Table 1. Area and Pressure of Boxes Weighing 2,600 N		
Box Number	Area of Bottom Side (m²)	Pressure (Pa)
1	3.0	867
2	2.6	1,000
3	?	1,182
4	1.8	1,444
5	1.4	?

The graph shows atmospheric pressure on Earth at several different altitudes above sea level.

Altitude and Atmospheric Pressure on Earth

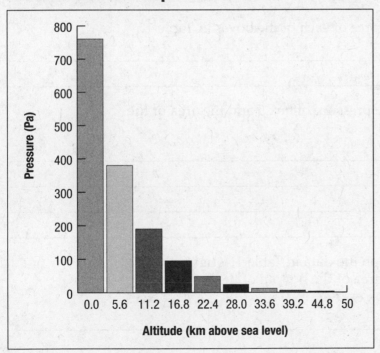

Name _____ Class _____ Date _____

Data about the atmosphere of Earth and its two closest neighboring planets in the solar system are given in Table 2.

Table 2. Atmosphere of Earth, Venus, and Mars		
Name of Planet	Composition of Atmosphere	Pressure of Atmosphere (kPa)
Earth	77% nitrogen 21% oxygen 1% argon 1% other	101
Venus	96% carbon dioxide 4% nitrogen 1% other	9120
Mars	95% carbon dioxide 3% nitrogen 2% argon	< 1

Questions

1. a. **Identifying** What is the force of each of the boxes in Table 1?

   _____
   _____

   b. **Calculating** Calculate the pressure of box 5 and the area of the bottom side of box 3.

   _____
   _____
   _____

   c. **Interpreting Data** Based on the data in Table 1, what is the relationship between the area of the bottom of the box and the amount of pressure the box exerts?

   _____
   _____
   _____

2. a. Describing From the graph, describe how atmospheric pressure changes with increasing distance above sea level.

_____

_____

_____

b. Predicting Predict what the atmospheric pressure is at 50 kilometers above sea level.

_____

_____

_____

c. Applying Concepts Explain why a balloon filled with air at sea level would expand in size as it rose to a higher altitude.

_____

_____

_____

_____

3. a. Identifying Which two planets in Table 2 are most similar in the composition of their atmosphere?

_____

_____

_____

b. Comparing and Contrasting Compare and contrast the atmospheric pressures of the three planets.

_____

_____

_____

_____

c. Relating Cause and Effect What factor(s) might explain the very different atmospheric pressures of Venus and Mars?

_____

_____

_____

_____

Chapter 14 Work, Power, and Machines

Section 14.1 Work and Power
(pages 412–416)

Math Skills **Work and Power**

Content and Vocabulary Support

What Is Work?
Work is the product of force and distance, or:

Work = Force × Distance

Work is measured in newton-meters (N·m), which are called joules (J).

What Is Power?
Power is the rate of doing work. Doing work at a faster rate requires more power. With more power, you can do more work in the same time or do the same amount of work in less time. For example, if you use a snowblower instead of a shovel, you can move more snow in the same amount of time, or you can move the same amount of snow in a shorter time. This is because the snowblower has more power.

Calculating Power
To calculate power, you divide the amount of work done by the time needed to do the work. The equation for power is:

$$Power = \frac{Work}{Time}$$

Time is measured in seconds (s). The unit of power is the **watt** (W). A watt equals one joule per second. For example, an 800-watt microwave uses 800 joules of power in one second.

Another common unit of power is the **horsepower** (hp). One horsepower equals about 746 watts. The horsepower of a lawnmower might be 4 hp, whereas the horsepower of a car might be 190 hp, or almost 142,000 watts of power.

Section 14.1 Work and Power

Solved Examples

Example 1: It takes 40 watts of power to operate a light bulb for 1 second. How much work does the light bulb do in that time?

Given: Power = 40 W
   Time = 1 s

Unknown: Work

Equation: Power = $\dfrac{\text{Work}}{\text{Time}}$

Solution: Solve the power equation for work:
   Work = Power × Time

Substitute the given values:

$$\text{Work} = \frac{40\ \text{W}}{1\ \text{s}} = \frac{40\ \text{J/s}}{1\ \text{s}} = 40\ \text{J}$$

Example 2: How much power is needed to lift a book to a height of 2.0 meters in a time of 1.0 second, if the book exerts a force of 20 newtons?

Given: Distance = 2.0 m
   Time = 1.0 s
   Force = 20 N

Unknown: Power

Equations: Power = $\dfrac{\text{Work}}{\text{Time}}$ and Work = Force × Distance

Solution: Find the value for work by substituting the given values for force and distance in the work equation:

$$\text{Work} = 20\ \text{N} \times 2.0\ \text{m} = 40\ \text{N·m} = 40\ \text{J}$$

Substitute the values for work and time in the power equation to find the value for power:

$$\text{Power} = \frac{40\ \text{J}}{1\ \text{s}} = 40\ \text{J/s} = 40\ \text{W}$$

Name _____ Class _____ Date _____

Practice Exercises

Exercise 1:   A light bulb does 100 joules of work in 2.5 seconds.
How much power does it have?

Exercise 2:   A man exerts 700 newtons of force to move a piece of
furniture 4 meters. If it takes him 2 seconds to move the
furniture, how much power does it require?

Exercise 3:   A hair curling iron uses 13 watts of power. How long
must it operate to do 1,040 joules of work?

Exercise 4:   A 4-watt night light is left on for 8 hours each night.
How much work does it do per night?

Exercise 5:   How much horsepower is needed to move a box that
has a force of 1,492 newtons a distance of 2 meters in
1 second?

Chapter 14   Work, Power, and Machines

Section 14.3 Mechanical Advantage and Efficiency

(pages 421–426)

Math Skills *Calculating Mechanical Advantage and Efficiency*

Content and Vocabulary Support

Mechanical Advantage

The input force of a machine is the force exerted on a machine, and the output force is the force produced by the machine. The number of times that a machine increases an input force to produce an output force is called its **mechanical advantage**. The higher the output force relative to the input force, the greater the mechanical advantage. There are two different types of mechanical advantage: actual mechanical advantage and ideal mechanical advantage.

Actual Mechanical Advantage

The **actual mechanical advantage** of a machine is determined by measuring the actual forces acting on the machine. It equals the ratio of output force to input force:

$$\text{Actual mechanical advantage (AMA)} = \frac{\text{Output force}}{\text{Input force}}$$

The actual mechanical advantage is a measure of the performance of the machine in the real world. It includes the effect of friction on mechanical advantage.

Ideal Mechanical Advantage

The **ideal mechanical advantage** of a machine is the mechanical advantage in the absence of friction. Ideal mechanical advantage equals the ratio of input distance to output distance:

$$\text{Ideal mechanical advantage (IMA)} = \frac{\text{Input distance}}{\text{Output distance}}$$

Recall that input distance is the distance through which the input force is exerted, and output distance is the distance through which the output force is exerted.

Because friction is always present, the actual mechanical advantage of a machine is always less than the ideal mechanical advantage. The greater the difference, the less efficient the machine.

Section 14.3 Mechanical Advantage and Efficiency

Efficiency

Because some of the work input to a machine is used to overcome friction, work output is always less than work input. The percent of work input that becomes work output is called **efficiency**. It is calculated by:

$$\text{Efficiency} = \frac{\text{Work ouput}}{\text{Work input}} \times 100\%$$

Due to friction, the efficiency of a machine is always less than 100 percent.

Solved Examples

Example 1:   Tamara rides her skateboard 1.5 meters up a ramp to a height of 0.5 meters above the ground. What is the ideal mechanical advantage of the ramp?

Given: Input distance = 1.5 m
　　　Output distance = 0.5 m

Unknown: Ideal mechanical advantage (IMA)

Equation: $\text{IMA} = \dfrac{\text{Input distance}}{\text{Output distance}}$

Solution: $\text{IMA} = \dfrac{1.5 \text{ m}}{0.5 \text{ m}} = 3$

Example 2:   What is the output distance of a machine with an input distance of 3.0 centimeters and an ideal mechanical advantage of 12?

Given: Input distance = 3.0 cm
　　　IMA = 6

Unknown: Output distance

Equation: $\text{IMA} = \dfrac{\text{Input distance}}{\text{Output distance}}$

Solution: Solve the equation for output distance, and substitute the given values:

$$\text{Output distance} = \frac{\text{Input distance}}{\text{IMA}};$$

$$\text{Output distance} = \frac{3 \text{ cm}}{12} = 0.25 \text{ cm}$$

Name _____ Class _____ Date _____

Example 3: A machine has a work output of 8 joules and requires 10 joules of work input to operate. What is the machine's efficiency?

Given: Work output = 8 J
Work input = 10 J

Unknown: Efficiency

Equation: Efficiency = $\dfrac{\text{Work output}}{\text{Work input}} \times 100\%$

Solution: Efficiency = $\dfrac{8\text{ J}}{10\text{ J}} \times 100\% = 80\%$

Example 4: What is the work output of a machine that has a work input of 2,800 joules and an efficiency of 92.3 percent?

Given: Work input: 2,800 J
Efficiency = 92.3%

Unknown: Work output

Equation: Efficiency = $\dfrac{\text{Work output}}{\text{Work input}}$

Solution: Solve the equation for work output:

Work output = Efficiency × Work input

Substitute the given values in this equation:

Work output = 92.5% × 2,800 J = 2,590 J

Practice Exercises

Exercise 1: A ski lift carries people along a 220-meter cable up the side of a mountain. Riders are lifted a total of 110 meters in elevation. What is the ideal mechanical advantage of the ski lift?

Exercise 2: The ideal mechanical advantage of a machine is 3.2 and its output distance is 2.5 meters. What is the input distance?

Physical Science Math Skills and Problem Solving Workbook **57**

Exercise 3: Paco rode his skateboard up a ramp for a distance of 3.8 meters. If the ideal mechanical advantage of the ramp is 2, how far above the ground was Paco?

Exercise 4: The inventor of a new machine claims that its actual mechanical advantage is 4. Literature on the machine reports its input distance is 81 meters and its output distance is 27 meters. Find the machine's ideal mechanical advantage, and determine whether the developer's claim could be true.

Exercise 5: What is the efficiency of a machine that has work input of 40 joules and work output of 35 joules?

Exercise 6: Work output of a large machine in a factory is 89,000 joules, and its input is 102,000 joules. Work output of a similar machine is 92,000 joules, and its work input is 104,000 joules. Which machine has greater efficiency?

Exercise 7: Lucas has been challenged to increase the efficiency of a device he is redesigning. His goal is 90 percent efficiency. The work input of the device is fixed at 10 joules, so Lucas is trying to improve work output. How many joules of work output should Lucas aim for to attain his goal of 90 percent efficiency?

Chapter 14   Work, Power, and Machines

Section 14.4 Simple Machines
(pages 427–437)

Data Analysis   *Analyzing Pulley Performance*

Content and Vocabulary Support

Pulleys

A pulley is one of six types of simple machines. A **pulley** is a simple machine that consists of a rope that fits into a groove in a wheel. It is used to lift objects. You may have used a pulley to raise a garage door, pull up a blind, or raise a flag.

There are three types of pulleys: fixed pulleys, movable pulleys, and pulley systems. They are shown in the diagram. Pulleys produce an output force that is different in size, direction, or both from the input force. Fixed pulleys change only the direction of the input force. Movable pulleys change both the direction and the size of the input force. Pulley systems are made up of combinations of fixed and movable pulleys, so they also change both the direction and the size of the input force.

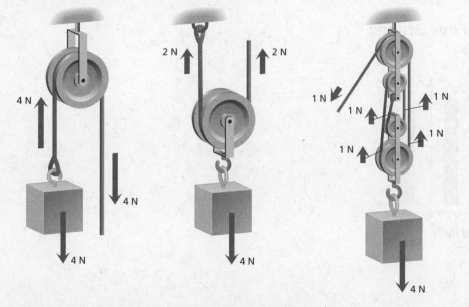

Ideal Mechanical Advantage of Pulleys

The ideal mechanical advantage of a pulley or pulley system is equal to the number of rope sections supporting the load being lifted. In a fixed pulley, only one rope section supports the load being lifted (see diagram). Therefore, the ideal mechanical advantage of a fixed pulley is 1. In a movable pulley, two rope sections support the load, so the ideal mechanical advantage is 2. A pulley system may have four or more rope sections supporting the load. The ideal mechanical advantage of a pulley system may therefore equal 4 or more.

Section 14.4 Simple Machines

Data

The table shows the output force and ideal mechanical advantage (IMA) of four different pulleys or pulley systems. All four pulleys or pulley systems have the same input force.

Output Force and IMA of Four Pulleys or Pulley Systems with an Input Force of 1,000 Newtons		
Pulley or Pulley System	Output Force (newtons, N)	IMA
A	850	1
B	1,970	2
C	3,680	4
D	5,740	6

The graph compares the actual mechanical advantage (AMA) and ideal mechanical advantage of four different brands of movable pulley.

AMA and IMA of Four Brands of Movable Pulley

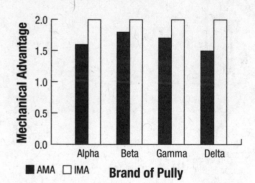

Questions

1. a. **Identifying** Based on the IMA values in the table, which type
   of pulley or pulley system is represented by each of the pulleys,
   A through D?

   _____

   _____

   _____

   b. **Calculating** Recall that the actual mechanical advantage of a
   machine is the ratio of output force to input force. What is the
   actual mechanical advantage of pulley D?

   _____

   _____

   _____

   c. **Explaining** Compare pulley D's actual mechanical advantage
   with its ideal mechanical advantage. Explain why the two types
   of mechanical advantage are not equal.

   _____

   _____

   _____

   _____

2. a. **Identifying** In the graph, which brand of pulley has the largest
   actual mechanical advantage? The smallest actual mechanical
   advantage?

   _____

   _____

   b. **Explaining** Why is the ideal mechanical advantage of each
   brand of pulley in the graph the same?

   _____

   _____

   _____

   c. **Interpreting Data** If the input force is the same for each type of
   pulley in the graph, which pulley has the greatest output force?
   Explain your answer.

   _____

   _____

   _____

Chapter 15   Energy

Section 15.1 Energy and Its Forms
(pages 446–452)

Math Skills *Calculating Kinetic Energy and Potential Energy*

Content and Vocabulary Support

Types of Energy

Energy is the ability to do work. There are many forms of energy, including mechanical energy and electrical energy. Many of the forms of energy can be classified into two general types: kinetic energy and potential energy.

Kinetic Energy

Kinetic energy is the energy of motion. The kinetic energy of any moving object depends on its mass and speed. The equation for calculating kinetic energy is:

$$\text{Kinetic energy (KE)} = \frac{1}{2}\,mv^2$$

Kinetic energy is measured in joules (J). The letter m represents the mass of the object, which is measured in kilograms. The letter v represents the object's speed, measured in meters per second (m/s).

From the equation, you can see that if you double the mass of an object, its kinetic energy doubles. If you double the speed of the object, its kinetic energy quadruples. Thus, speed has a greater impact on kinetic energy than does mass.

Potential Energy

Potential energy is energy that is stored as a result of position or shape. In other words, it is energy with the potential to do work. For example, potential energy is stored in the stretched strings of a guitar. It is also stored in the leaves high on a tree. If the string is plucked or the leaves fall, the potential energy turns into kinetic energy.

Any object raised above the ground has potential energy due to gravity. This type of potential energy is called **gravitational potential energy**. It depends on an object's height as well as its mass. The equation for gravitational potential energy is:

$$\text{Potential energy (PE)} = mgh$$

Potential energy is measured in joules. The letter m represents mass (kg), and g represents acceleration due to gravity ($9.8\ \text{m/s}^2$). The product mg gives the weight of the object. The letter h represents the object's height above the ground.

Section 15.1 Energy and Its Forms

An object at ground level has a gravitational potential energy of zero, no matter how great its mass. At a height of 1 meter, a 1-kilogram object has potential energy of:

$$PE = 1 \text{ kg} \times 9.8 \text{ m/s}^2 \times 1 \text{ m} = 9.8 \text{ J}$$

Doubling either the mass or the height of the object will double its gravitational potential energy. Thus, mass and height have an equal impact on gravitational potential energy.

Solved Examples

Example 1: A bicycle and rider with a combined mass of 110 kilograms are traveling at a speed of 8 meters per second. What is the kinetic energy of the bicycle and rider?

Given: $m = 110 \text{ kg}$
$v = 8 \text{ m/s}$

Unknown: Kinetic energy (KE)

Equation: $KE = \frac{1}{2} mv^2$

Solution: $KE = \frac{1}{2} \times 110 \text{ kg} \times (8 \text{ m/s})^2 = 3{,}520 \text{ J}$

Example 2: The kinetic energy of a bowling ball traveling at a speed of 4 meters per second is 50 joules. Find the mass of the ball.

Given: $KE = 50 \text{ J}$
$v = 4 \text{ m/s}$

Unknown: Mass (m)

Equation: $KE = \frac{1}{2} mv^2$

Solution: Solve the equation for m:

$$m = \frac{2 \, KE}{v^2}$$

Substitute the given values in this equation:

$$m = \frac{2 \times 50 \text{ J}}{(4 \text{ m/s})^2} = 6.25 \text{ kg}$$

Name _____ Class _____ Date _____

Example 3: What is the gravitational potential energy of a 5-kilogram object resting at a height of 3 meters off the ground?

Given: $m = 5$ kg
$h = 3$ m
$g = 9.8$ m/s^2

Unknown: Gravitational potential energy (PE)

Equation: PE $= mgh$

Solution: PE $= 5$ kg $\times 9.8$ m/s$^2 \times 3$ m $= 147$ J

Example 4: The gravitational potential energy of a 15-kilogram object is 294 joules. What is the height of the object above the ground?

Given: PE $= 294$ J
$m = 15$ kg
$g = 9.8$ m/s^2

Unknown: Height (h)

Equation: PE $= mgh$

Solution: Solve the equation for h, and then substitute the given values in the new equation:

$$h = \frac{\text{PE}}{mg}; h = \frac{294 \text{ J}}{15 \text{ kg} \times 9.8 \text{ m/s}^2} = 2.0 \text{ m}$$

Practice Exercises

Exercise 1: Find the kinetic energy of a 0.1-kilogram toy truck moving at a speed of 1.1 meters per second.

Exercise 2: What is the speed of a 48-kilogram dog running across a lawn with 216 joules of kinetic energy?

Exercise 3: A book on a shelf 2.0 meters above the floor has a mass of 1.5 kilograms. What is the gravitational potential energy of the book?

Exercise 4: Find the mass of a ball on a roof 30 meters high, if the ball's gravitational potential energy is 58.8 joules.

Exercise 5: Which runner has greater kinetic energy: a 46-kilogram runner moving at a speed of 8 meters per second or a 92-kilogram runner moving at a speed of 4 meters per second?

Exercise 6: If a 6-kilogram box is moved from the floor to a storage compartment 2 meters above the floor, by how many joules does its gravitational potential energy change?

Exercise 7: A 0.1-kilogram ball rolls across the floor at a speed of 2 meters per second. Another 0.1-kilogram ball rests on a shelf 1 meter above the floor. Which ball has more energy?

Name _____ Class _____ Date _____

Section 15.2 Energy Conversion and Conservation

(pages 453–461)

⬥ **Math** **Skills** *Using the Law of Conservation of Energy*

Content and Vocabulary Support

Energy Conversion and Conservation

Energy can be changed from one form to another. The process of
changing energy from one form to another is called **energy
conversion**. For example, a light bulb changes electrical energy into
thermal energy (heat) and electromagnetic energy (light). The law of
conservation of energy states that energy cannot be created or
destroyed. Thus, when energy changes from one form to another, the
amount of energy remains the same.

Examples of Energy Conversion

One of the most common energy conversions is between potential
energy and kinetic energy. Whenever an object falls, the gravitational
potential energy of the object is converted to the kinetic energy of
motion. When a spring is released, it also results in the conversion of
potential energy to kinetic energy.

   The swinging of a pendulum and the movement of a pole vaulter
are other examples of kinetic and potential energy conversions. When
a pendulum swings from side to side, it has kinetic energy. At the
high point of each swing, the pendulum momentarily stops. At that
point it has gravitational potential energy but no kinetic energy. Then
it swings in the opposite direction, and its potential energy is
converted to kinetic energy again. A pole vaulter runs and uses her
pole to gain kinetic energy that helps propel her into the air. In the air,
she has gravitational potential energy. As she falls back to the ground,
her potential energy is converted back to kinetic energy.

Conservation of Mechanical Energy

Recall that mechanical energy is the total kinetic and potential energy
of an object.

   Mechanical energy = KE + PE

Because of the law of conservation of energy, total mechanical energy
remains constant. This can be written as:

   $(KE + PE)_{beginning} = (KE + PE)_{end}$

Section 15.2 Energy Conversion and Conservation

Solved Examples

Example 1: A 1.25-kilogram stone fell from a cliff and struck the ground at a speed of 29.4 meters per second. What was the gravitational potential energy of the stone before it fell?

Given: $m = 1.25$ kg $\quad v = 29.4$ m/s

Unknown: $PE_{beginning}$ $\quad KE_{beginning}$ $\quad PE_{end}$ $\quad KE_{end}$

Equations: $KE = \frac{1}{2} mv^2$ and $(KE + PE)_{beginning} = (KE + PE)_{end}$

Solution: The stone has no kinetic energy until it starts to fall, so $KE_{beginning}$ equals zero. After the stone lands on the ground, it no longer has potential energy, so PE_{end} equals zero. Calculate KE_{end} using the first equation and given values:

$$KE_{end} = \frac{1}{2} \times 1.25 \text{ kg} \times (29.4 \text{ m/s})^2 = 540 \text{ J}$$

Substitute the known values into the second equation, and solve for $PE_{beginning}$:

$$0 + PE_{beginning} = 540 \text{ J} + 0; PE_{beginning} = 540 \text{ J}$$

Example 2: A 56-kilogram teen attached to a bungee cord jumps off a 10-meter-high tower. What is her kinetic energy when she reaches the bottom of her fall?

Given: $m = 56$ kg $\quad h = 10$ m

Unknown: KE_{end} $\quad PE_{beginning}$ $\quad KE_{beginning}$ $\quad PE_{end}$

Equations: $PE = mgh$ and $(KE + PE)_{beginning} = (KE + PE)_{end}$

Solution: By the same reasoning as in Example 1, $KE_{beginning}$ and PE_{end} equal zero. Calculate $PE_{beginning}$ using the first equation and given values:

$$PE_{beginning} = 56 \text{ kg} \times 9.8 \text{ m/s}^2 \times 10 \text{ m} = 5,488 \text{ J}$$

Substitute the known values into the second equation, and solve for KE_{end}:

$$0 + 5,488 \text{ J} = KE_{end} + 0; KE_{end} = 5,488 \text{ J}$$

Practice Exercises

Exercise 1: A book with 67 joules of gravitational potential energy fell from a shelf and landed on the floor. What was its kinetic energy when it landed on the floor?

Exercise 2: A 0.2-kilogram object is lifted into the air and then dropped to the floor. If it is moving at a speed of 3 meters per second when it hits the floor, what was its gravitational potential energy before it was dropped?

Exercise 3: Lance threw a ball straight up into the air. The ball's gravitational potential energy at its peak height was 0.4 joules, and its speed when it hit the ground was 4 meters per second. What was the mass of the ball?

Exercise 4: Alfredo, who has a mass of 60 kilograms, jumped off a retaining wall. His kinetic energy when he landed on the ground was 882 joules. How high was the wall?

Exercise 5: A water feature in a garden recycles water with a pump. Water is pumped from a stone basin up through a pipe 1 meter high. At that height, the water flows out through a tap and falls down through the air to the basin below, where the cycle begins again. What is the gravitational potential energy of 2.5 kilograms of water at the top of the pipe? How fast is the falling water moving by the time it reaches the basin?

Chapter 15   Energy

Section 15.3 Energy Resources
(pages 462–466)

Data **Analysis** *Analyzing Energy Use*

Content and Vocabulary Support

Energy Resources

We all depend on energy resources as we go through each day. We use electricity made from burning coal to power our lights and appliances. We use natural gas to heat our homes and gasoline made from oil to run our cars. All these energy resources, as well as others, can be classified as either renewable or nonrenewable.

Nonrenewable Energy Resources

Nonrenewable energy resources are resources that exist in limited quantities. Once used, these resources cannot be replaced for millions of years. Nonrenewable energy resources include oil, natural gas, and coal.

Oil, natural gas, and coal are also called **fossil fuels**. At present, most of the energy used worldwide comes from fossil fuels. These fuels are not distributed evenly around the world. For example, more than half the world's known oil supply is located in a small area of the Middle East. Nonetheless, fossil fuels are relatively cheap and usually readily available. However, using them creates pollution.

Renewable Energy Resources

Renewable energy resources are resources that can be replaced in a relatively short period of time. Most renewable energy resources come directly or indirectly from the sun. Generally, using them creates less pollution than the use of fossil fuels. Renewable energy resources include hydroelectric, solar, geothermal, wind, and biomass resources.

Hydroelectric energy is electric energy obtained from the kinetic energy of flowing water. **Solar energy** is energy that comes directly from sunlight. **Geothermal energy** is the heat that lies beneath Earth's surface. The heat can be tapped to produce electricity. **Biomass energy** is the chemical energy stored in living things. Burning wood is an example of the use of biomass energy.

A recently developed source of renewable energy is the hydrogen fuel cell. A **hydrogen fuel cell** generates electricity by reacting hydrogen with oxygen. In the future, nuclear fusion may also be used as a renewable energy resource.

Section 15.3 Energy Resources

Data

The graph compares the percentages of different types of energy resources used in the world and in the United States in 1998.

Use of Energy Resources by Type in 1998, Worldwide and United States

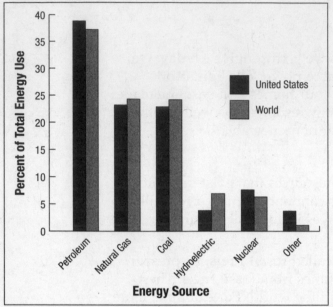

The table shows the population and energy use of several countries and regions of the world in 1998, as a percentage of world totals.

Population and Energy Use in Countries and Regions of the World, 1998		
Country or Region	*Percent of World Population*	*Percent of World Energy Use*
United States	4.6	24.4
Canada	0.5	3.2
Mexico	1.7	1.5
Central and South America	6.7	4.8
Western Europe	7.2	17.5
Eastern Europe and Russia	6.9	14.0
Middle East	3.7	4.6
Africa	13.0	3.3
East Asia, Australia, and Oceania	53.6	20.7
Japan	2.2	5.9

Name _____ Class _____ Date _____

Questions

1. a. **Observing** In the graph, which single energy source supplied nearly 40 percent of the energy used in the United States and the world in 1998?

_____

_____

   b. **Interpreting Data** Which three sources of energy contributed more to energy use worldwide than they did to energy use in the United States? Which one energy source was used almost twice as much worldwide as it was in the United States?

_____

_____

_____

   c. **Comparing and Contrasting** How did the use of fossil fuels in the United States compare with their use worldwide in 1998?

_____

_____

_____

2. a. **Listing** From the table, list the two countries or regions that had the largest percentages of world energy use in 1998.

_____

_____

   b. **Calculating** Calculate the ratio of percent of world energy use to percent of world population for these two countries or regions. Which country or region used more energy per person?

_____

_____

_____

   c. **Interpreting Data** Three fourths of the world's population lives in Mexico, Central and South America, Africa, East Asia, Australia and Oceania. What percentage of the world's energy is used by these countries and regions combined?

_____

_____

_____

_____

Section 16.1 Thermal Energy and Matter

(pages 474–478)

Math Skills *Calculations Using Specific Heat*

Content and Vocabulary Support

Heat and Temperature

Heat is the transfer of thermal energy from one object to another because of a temperature difference. Heat flows spontaneously from hot objects to cold objects. This flow of heat is the reason a hot object feels hot. Heat flows from the object to your cooler hands when you touch it.

Temperature is a measure of how hot or cold an object is, compared to a reference point. On the Celsius scale, there are two reference points: the freezing and boiling points of water. On the Kelvin scale, the reference point is absolute zero.

Thermal Energy and Thermal Expansion

Recall that thermal energy is the total potential and kinetic energy of all the particles in an object. The thermal energy of an object depends on its mass, temperature, and phase (solid, liquid, or gas). The larger the mass, the greater the thermal energy. For example, a pot of coffee has more mass than a cup of coffee, so its thermal energy is greater. Objects with higher temperature also have greater thermal energy. A cup of hot coffee has more thermal energy than a cup of cold milk.

Thermal expansion is an increase in the volume of a material due to a temperature increase. Thermal expansion occurs when particles of matter move farther apart as they gain heat. Thermal expansion is greater in gases than in liquids or solids, because the forces of attraction among gas particles are weaker. The opposite process, thermal contraction, occurs when temperature decreases. Particles of matter move closer together as they lose heat, and volume decreases.

Specific Heat

Specific heat is the amount of heat needed to raise the temperature of one gram of a material by one degree Celsius. It is measured in joules per gram per degree Celsius, or J/g·°C. The lower a material's specific heat, the more its temperature rises when a given amount of energy is absorbed by a given mass of the material.

The amount of heat (Q) absorbed by an object depends on its mass (m), the specific heat (c) of its material, and the change in temperature (ΔT). The amount of heat can be calculated with the equation:

$$Q = m \times c \times \Delta T$$

Section 16.1 Thermal Energy and Matter

Solved Examples

Example 1: A plastic spoon has a mass of 10 grams. The specific heat of the plastic in the spoon is 2.00 J/g·°C. How much heat must be absorbed by the spoon to raise its temperature by 2°C?

Given: Mass (m) = 10 g
Specific heat (c) = 2.00 J/g·°C
Temperature change (ΔT) = 2°C

Unknown: Amount of heat (Q)

Equation: $Q = m \times c \times \Delta T$

Solution: $Q = 10\text{g} \times 2.00 \text{ J/g·°C} \times 2\text{°C} = 40 \text{ J}$

Example 2: It takes 1,077.6 joules of heat to change the temperature of an iron nail by 80°C. If the specific heat of iron is 0.449 J/g·°C, what is the mass of the nail?

Given: Amount of heat (Q) = 1,077.6 J
Temperature change (ΔT) = 80°C
Specific heat (c) = 0.449 J/g·°C

Unknown: Mass (m)

Equation: $Q = m \times c \times \Delta T$

Solution: Solve the equation for mass:

$$m = \frac{Q}{c \times \Delta T}$$

Substitute the given values into this equation:

$$m = \frac{1,077.6 \text{ J}}{0.449 \text{ J/g·°C} \times 80\text{°C}} = 30 \text{ g}$$

Example 3: A 7.0-gram ring absorbs 4.9 joules of heat. If the temperature of the ring increases 3.0°C, what is the ring's specific heat?

Given: Mass (m) = 7.0 g
Temperature change (ΔT) = 3.0°C
Amount of heat (Q) = 4.9 J

Unknown: Specific heat (c)

Equation: $Q = m \times c \times \Delta T$

Solution: Solve the equation for specific heat:

$$c = \frac{Q}{m \times \Delta T}$$

Substitute the given values into this equation:

$$c = \frac{49 \text{ J}}{7.0 \text{ J} \times 3.0\text{°C}} = 0.23 \text{ J/g·°C}$$

Name _____ Class _____ Date _____

Practice Exercises

Exercise 1:   The specific heat of silver is 0.235 J/g·°C. How much heat is needed to raise the temperature of an 8-gram silver ring by 50°C?

Exercise 2:   Tori wants to increase the temperature of 500 grams of water from 20°C to 100°C. If the specific heat of water is 4.18 J/g·°C, how much heat is needed?

Exercise 3:   Gold has a specific heat of 0.130 J/g·°C. If 195 joules of heat are added to 15 grams of gold, how much does the temperature of the gold change?

Exercise 4:   A plastic container with a mass of 30 grams gains 1,140 joules of heat. If the temperature of the container increases 20°C, what is the specific heat of the plastic in the container?

Exercise 5:   A silver coin and a gold coin each have a mass of exactly 6.6 grams. The specific heat of silver is 0.235 J/g·°C, and the specific heat of gold is 0.130 J/g·°C. Which coin requires more heat to raise its temperature by 40°C?

Chapter 16 Thermal Energy and Heat

Section 16.3 Using Heat
(pages 486–492)

Data Analysis **Analyzing Heating and Cooling Systems**

Content and Vocabulary Support

Heating Systems

In the United States today, most homes are heated with a central heating system. A **central heating system** heats many rooms from one central location. The central location often is in the basement. Central heating systems differ in the type of energy source they use. The most common energy sources for central heating systems are electricity, natural gas, oil, and coal.

Types of central heating systems include hot-water, steam, electric baseboard, and forced air heating systems. In a hot-water heating system, water is heated in a boiler and then pumped to radiators in each room. As the radiator pipes heat up, they heat the air near them by conduction and radiation. A convection current then carries the heat throughout each room.

Steam heating is similar to hot-water heating, except that steam is used instead of hot water. In electric baseboard heating, electricity heats a coil in a baseboard unit. The hot coil heats the air near it by conduction and radiation. A convection current then circulates warm air throughout the room. In forced-air heating, fans circulate warm air though ducts to the rooms. Then, a convection current circulates the warm air within each room.

Cooling Systems

Most cooling systems, such as refrigerators and air conditioners, are heat pumps. A **heat pump** is a device that reverses the normal flow of thermal energy. Instead of heat moving from a warmer to a cooler object or room, with the help of a heat pump, heat moves from a cooler to a warmer object or room.

In a heat pump, an electric motor circulates a refrigerant through tubing under pressure. A **refrigerant** is a fluid that vaporizes and condenses with changes of pressure inside the tubing of a heat pump. When the refrigerant vaporizes, or turns into a gas, it absorbs heat. When the refrigerant condenses, or turns back into a liquid, it gives off heat. In a refrigerator, the refrigerant absorbs heat from inside the cold refrigerator and gives it off to the warmer room. In an air conditioner, the refrigerant absorbs heat from inside a cool room and gives it off to the warmer air outside the house.

Section 16.3 Using Heat

Data

The table shows the approximate cost per hour of electricity needed
to operate various home appliances that involve heating or cooling.
The cost is computed by multiplying the amount of energy needed to
operate the appliance for one hour by a constant hourly rate for
electricity.

Hourly Cost of Operating Home Appliances	
Appliance	Cost ($/hour)
Window air conditioner	0.15
Ceiling fan	0.03
Refrigerator	0.02
Conventional oven	0.15
Microwave oven	0.12
Toaster oven	0.10
Clothes iron	0.08
Hair dryer	0.08
Waterbed heater	0.01
Water heater	0.05

The graph shows the annual energy cost of operating central heating
systems that use different types of energy sources.

Annual Energy Cost of Heating Systems

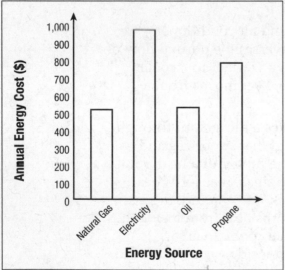

Questions

1. a. Listing From the table, list the appliances that cost less than the $0.05 per hour to operate. List those that cost more than $0.10 per hour to operate.

_____

_____

_____

b. Inferring Which appliance uses more electrical energy per hour, a window air conditioner or a microwave oven? Explain your answer.

_____

_____

_____

c. Problem Solving In addition to the cost per hour, what other information do you need to know in order to calculate the total cost of operating an appliance?

_____

_____

_____

2. a. Identifying In the graph, identify which type of heating source costs the most to use and which costs the least.

_____

_____

b. Calculating How much more per year does it cost to use the most expensive heating source than the least expensive source?

_____

_____

_____

c. Making Judgments In addition to the type of energy source and its cost, what other factors might home owners consider when deciding which type of heating system is the best choice for them?

_____

_____

_____

_____

_____

Section 17.2 Properties of Mechanical Waves

(pages 504–507)

Math > Skills *Calculating the Speed of Mechanical Waves*

Content and Vocabulary Support

Period, Frequency, and Wavelength

Any motion that repeats at regular time intervals is called **periodic motion**. An example of periodic motion is an ocean wave. One complete motion that returns to its starting point is called a cycle. The time needed for one cycle is called the **period**. The **frequency** of a periodic motion is the number of cycles in a given time. Frequency is measured in cycles per second, or **hertz** (Hz). The frequency of the vibrating source producing a wave determines the wave's frequency.

Wavelength, usually measured in meters, is the distance between a point on a wave and the same point on the next cycle of the wave. For transverse waves, wavelength is the distance between adjacent crests or troughs. For longitudinal waves, wavelength is the distance between adjacent compressions or rarefactions. Increasing the frequency of a wave decreases its wavelength. In other words, when wavelength is shorter, crests or compressions are closer together.

Wave Speed

Recall that you can calculate the speed of a moving object by dividing the distance it travels by the time it takes to travel that distance. In a similar way, you can calculate the speed of a wave. Wave speed is wavelength divided by period:

$$\text{Speed} = \frac{\text{Wavelength}}{\text{Period}}$$

Because period is the inverse of frequency (Period $= \frac{1}{\text{Frequency}}$), you can also calculate the speed of a wave by multiplying its wavelength by its frequency:

$$\text{Speed} = \text{Wavelength} \times \text{Frequency}$$

Knowing any two variables in one of the speed equations allows you to find the third variable.

Section 17.2 Properties of Mechanical Waves

Solved Examples

Example 1: A wave in a spring has a wavelength of 0.1 meters and a period of 0.2 seconds. What is the speed of the wave?

Given: Wavelength = 0.1 m
Period = 0.2 s

Unknown: Speed

Equation: Speed = $\dfrac{\text{Wavelength}}{\text{Period}}$

Solution: Speed = $\dfrac{0.1\text{ m}}{0.2\text{ s}}$ = 0.5 m/s

Example 2: What is the speed of an ocean wave that has a wavelength of 4.0 meters and a frequency of 0.5 hertz?

Given: Wavelength = 4.0 m
Frequency = 0.5 Hz

Unknown: Speed

Equation: Speed = Wavelength × Frequency

Solution: Speed = 4.0 m × 0.5 Hz = 2.0 m/s

Example 3: Find the wavelength of a wave in a rope that has a frequency of 2.0 hertz and a speed of 0.4 meters per second.

Given: Frequency = 2.0 Hz
Speed = 0.4 m/s

Unknown: Wavelength

Equation: Speed = Wavelength × Frequency

Solution: Solve the equation for wavelength:

$$\text{Wavelength} = \frac{\text{Speed}}{\text{Frequency}}$$

Substitute the given values:

$$\text{Wavelength} = \frac{0.4\text{ m/s}}{2.0\text{ Hz}}$$

Practice Exercises

Exercise 1: What is the speed of an ocean wave that has a wavelength of 0.30 meters and a frequency of 1.80 hertz?

Exercise 2: Calculate the frequency of a wave in a spring toy. The wave has a speed of 1.1 meters per second and a wavelength of 0.1 meters.

Exercise 3: A wave ripples through a large flag when the wind blows steadily. What is the wavelength of the wave if its frequency is 12.0 hertz and its speed is 1.2 meters per second?

Exercise 4: If a wave in a long rope has a period of 1.0 second and a wavelength of 0.2 meters, what is its speed?

Exercise 5: What is the period of a wave generated by an earthquake, if it has a wavelength of 500 meters and a speed of 5,000 meters per second?

Chapter 18 The Electromagnetic Spectrum and Light

Section 18.1 Electromagnetic Waves
(pages 532–538)

Math Skills *Calculating the Speed of Electromagnetic Waves*

Content and Vocabulary Support

What Are Electromagnetic Waves?

Electromagnetic waves are invisible transverse waves that are produced when an electric charge vibrates or accelerates. They consist of constantly changing electric and magnetic fields. An **electric field** is a field that exerts electric forces on charged particles. A **magnetic field** is a field that exerts magnetic forces on charged particles. In electromagnetic waves, the electric and magnetic fields are at right angles to each other and to the direction of the wave, as shown in the diagram below. Examples of electromagnetic waves include radio waves, light waves, and X-rays.

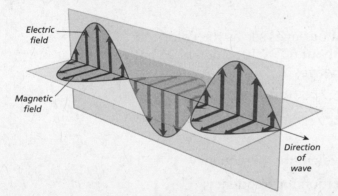

Like mechanical waves, electromagnetic waves carry energy from place to place. The transfer of energy by electromagnetic waves is called **electromagnetic radiation**. Unlike mechanical waves, electromagnetic waves can travel through a vacuum, or empty space, as well as through a medium.

Speed of Electromagnetic Waves

Light and all other electromagnetic waves travel at the same speed in a vacuum: 3.00×10^8 meters per second. The speed of light and other electromagnetic waves can be represented by the same equation that represents the speed of mechanical waves:

Speed = Wavelength × Frequency

Although all electromagnetic waves have the same speed, they may have different wavelengths and frequencies. If you know either the wavelength or the frequency of an electromagnetic wave, you can calculate the other variable using the speed equation and the known value for speed.

Section 18.1 Electromagnetic Waves

Solved Examples

Example 1: The frequency of the wave broadcast by a radio station is 1.2×10^6 hertz. What is the wavelength of the station's wave?

Given: Frequency = 1.2×10^6 Hz
Speed = 3.00×10^8 m/s

Unknown: Wavelength

Equation: Speed = Wavelength × Frequency

Solution: Solve the equation for wavelength:

$$\text{Wavelength} = \frac{\text{Speed}}{\text{Frequency}}$$

Substitute the given values:

$$\text{Wavelength} = \frac{3.00 \times 10^8 \text{ m/s}}{1.2 \times 10^6 \text{/s}} = 2.5 \times 10^2 \text{ m}$$

Example 2: Visible light waves that our eyes see as the color red have a wavelength of about 6.7×10^{-7} meters. What is the frequency of these waves?

Given: Wavelength = 6.7×10^{-7} m
Speed = 3.00×10^8 m/s

Unknown: Frequency

Equation: Speed = Wavelength × Frequency

Solution: Solve the equation for frequency:

$$\text{Frequency} = \frac{\text{Speed}}{\text{Wavelength}}$$

Substitute the given values:

$$\text{Frequency} = \frac{3.00 \times 10^8 \text{ m/s}}{6.7 \times 10^{-7} \text{ m}} = 4.5 \times 10^{15} \text{/s}$$

$$= 4.5 \times 10^{15} \text{ Hz}$$

Name _____ Class _____ Date _____

Practice Exercises

Exercise 1: The frequency of a microwave is 1.2×10^9 hertz. What is its wavelength?

Exercise 2: What is the frequency of an X-ray that has a wavelength of 1.5×10^{-9} meters?

Exercise 3: You cannot see high-frequency ultraviolet light rays, but they can damage your eyes and skin. Calculate the frequency of an ultraviolet light wave that has a wavelength of 3.0×10^{-7} meters.

Exercise 4: A radio station broadcasts a wave at a frequency of 1.0×10^6 hertz. What is its wavelength?

Exercise 5: A satellite transmits a radio wave with a wavelength of 5.0×10^5 meters. Calculate the frequency of the wave.

Section 18.2 The Electromagnetic Spectrum

(pages 539–545)

 *Analyzing Frequency and Wavelength of Electromagnetic Waves*

Content and Vocabulary Support

The Waves of the Electromagnetic Spectrum

The full range of frequencies of electromagnetic radiation is called the **electromagnetic spectrum.** The electromagnetic spectrum includes radio waves, infrared rays, visible light, ultraviolet rays, X-rays, and gamma rays. Wave frequency increases and wavelength decreases across the spectrum, from radio waves to gamma rays. In other words, the waves become faster and shorter.

Radio Waves

Radio waves have the lowest frequencies and longest wavelengths in the electromagnetic spectrum. Radio waves are used in radio, television, microwave ovens, and radar.

Infrared Rays

Infrared rays come next in the electromagnetic spectrum. They fall between radio waves and visible light in their frequencies and wavelengths. Infrared rays are used as a source of heat and to discover areas of heat differences.

Visible Light

Next in the spectrum is visible light. This is a very narrow range of frequencies and wavelengths that the human eye can see. Within this range, different wavelengths are seen by the human eye as different colors. People use visible light to see, keep safe, and communicate.

Ultraviolet Rays

The frequencies of ultraviolet rays are greater and the wavelengths shorter than for visible light. Ultraviolet rays help your skin produce vitamin D. In excess, they can burn the skin and cause skin cancer.

X-Rays and Gamma Rays

X-rays have higher frequencies and shorter wavelengths than ultraviolet rays. X-rays are used in medicine, industry, and transportation to make pictures of the inside of solid objects. Gamma rays have the highest frequencies and shortest wavelengths in the entire electromagnetic spectrum. Gamma rays are used to kill cancer cells.

Name _____ Class _____ Date _____

Section 18.2 The Electromagnetic Spectrum

Data

In the United States, the Federal Communications Commission decides which frequencies of radio waves can be used for different purposes. Table 1 shows the frequencies assigned to some of the different uses of radio waves.

Table 1. Frequencies of Radio Waves Assigned to Different Uses	
Frequency or Frequency Band (Hz)	Use
5.35×10^5 to 1.7×10^6	AM radio stations
5.9×10^6 to 2.61×10^7	Short-wave radio stations
2.696×10^7 to 2.741×10^7	Citizen band (CB) radio sets
4.0×10^7	Garage door openers
4.9×10^7	Baby monitors
4.0×10^7 to 5.0×10^7	Cordless telephones
5.4×10^7 to 8.8×10^7	Television stations, channels 2–6
8.8×10^7 to 1.08×10^8	FM radio stations
1.7×10^8 to 2.2×10^8	Television stations, channels 7–13
9.6×10^8 to 1.2×10^9	Air traffic control radar systems
1.227×10^9 to 1.575×10^9	Global positioning systems

Table 2 shows the wavelengths of different types of electromagnetic waves. For purposes of comparison, the table also lists objects or organisms that have the same lengths or diameters as the lengths of the waves.

Table 2. Wavelengths of Electromagnetic Waves		
Type of EM Waves	Wavelength (m)	Object or Organism Similar in Length or Diameter
Radio waves	$100 = 10^2$	Soccer field
Radio waves	$10 = 10^1$	House
Radio waves	$0.1 = 10^{-1}$	Baseball
Radio waves	$0.001 = 10^{-3}$	This period .
Infrared rays	$0.0001 = 10^{-4}$	Cell
Infrared rays	$0.000001 = 10^{-6}$	Bacterium
Ultraviolet rays	$0.0000001 = 10^{-7}$	Virus
X-rays	$0.00000001 = 10^{-8}$	Protein molecule
X-rays	$0.0000000001 = 10^{-10}$	Water molecule

Questions

1. a. **Classifying** The frequencies of radio waves in the electromagnetic spectrum range from 10^2 to 10^9 hertz. Waves with frequencies of 10^6 and higher are classified as high-frequency radio waves. Waves with frequencies below 10^6 are classified as low-frequency radio waves. Which use of radio waves in Table 1 uses radio waves classified as low-frequency?

——————————————————————————————

——————————————————————————————

b. **Inferring** The call number of a radio station is the frequency of its wave in megahertz (1 megahertz = 1 million hertz = 1×10^6 hertz). If a radio station's call number is 97.1, what is its frequency in hertz? Based on Table 1, is the radio station an AM or FM radio station? Explain your answer.

——————————————————————————————

——————————————————————————————

——————————————————————————————

c. **Applying Concepts** Explain why it might be possible to hear telephone conversations through a baby monitor.

——————————————————————————————

——————————————————————————————

——————————————————————————————

2. a. **Interpreting Tables** Based on the information in Table 2, name an object that might be about as long as an electromagnetic wave with a wavelength of 0.01 (10^{-2}) meters.

——————————————————————————————

——————————————————————————————

b. **Calculating** Recall that the product of wavelength and frequency of an electromagnetic wave equals its speed of 3.00×10^8 meters per second. What is the frequency of an infrared ray with a wavelength of 1.0×10^{-4} meters? Of 1.0×10^{-6} meters?

——————————————————————————————

——————————————————————————————

c. **Applying Concepts** The energy of electromagnetic waves varies inversely with their wavelength. How does the energy of an X-ray compare with the energy of a radio wave?

——————————————————————————————

——————————————————————————————

Chapter 19 Optics

Section 19.2 Lenses
(pages 574–578)

Data Analysis *Analyzing Refraction of Light*

Content and Vocabulary Support

Light Refraction

In a vacuum, light travels at a speed of 3.00×10^8 meters per second. Once light passes from a vacuum into any other medium, it slows down. The speed of light in the new medium depends on the material of the new medium. Light travels through air almost as fast as it travels through a vacuum. It travels much more slowly through water or glass.

Light usually travels in straight lines. When light enters a new medium at an angle, the change in speed occurs in one side of the wave before it occurs in the other side of the wave. This causes the light to bend. The bending of light is called refraction. The amount of bending that occurs depends on how much the speed of light changes as it goes from one medium to another. This, in turn, depends on the medium's index of refraction.

Index of Refraction

The **index of refraction** for a material is the ratio of the speed of light in a vacuum to the speed of light in the material. This can be represented by the equation:

$$\text{Index of refraction} = \frac{\text{Speed of light in a vacuum}}{\text{Speed of light in the material}}$$

The speed of light in a vacuum is always 3.00×10^8. The speed of light in any material is always slower, or less than 3.00×10^8. Therefore, the index of refraction is always a positive number greater than 1.

A material with a low index of refraction (near 1) causes light to slow and bend very little. For example, the index of refraction of air is only about 1.0003. This causes very little refraction. A material with a high index of refraction causes light to slow and bend much more. An example of a material with a very high index of refraction is the synthetic gemstone moissanite. It has an index of refraction of 2.65.

Section 19.2 Lenses

Data

Table 1 shows the index of refraction of many different materials, ranging from air, which has the lowest index of refraction, to diamond, which has a high index of refraction.

Table 1. Index of Refraction of Selected Materials	
Material	*Index*
Air	1.0003
Ice	1.31
Water (at 20°C)	1.33
Acetone	1.36
Ethyl alcohol	1.36
Sugar solution (30%)	1.38
Sugar solution (80%)	1.49
Flint glass	1.57–1.75
Sapphire	1.77
Arsenic trisulfide glass	2.04
Diamond	2.42

To determine the index of refraction of an unknown material, a powder of the material is mixed with immersion oil and examined under a light microscope. If the index of refraction of the powder is higher than the known index of refraction of the oil, the grains of powder will appear to have lines of light around them rather than an even distribution of light. The lines of light are due to the greater refraction of light occurring at the surface of the powder grains. Table 2 shows observations of mixtures of an unknown glass powder and oils with different indexes of refraction.

Table 2. Determining the Index of Refraction of an Unknown Glass	
Index of Refraction of Immersion Oil	*Observations of Immersion Oil/ Glass-Powder Mixture*
1.530	Bright lines of light around grains of powder
1.540	Bright lines of light around grains of powder
1.545	Bright lines of light around grains of powder
1.575	Lines of light very clear
1.600	Lines of light still clearly visible
1.610	Lines of light visible
1.620	Lines of light growing dimmer
1.630	Lines of light very faint
1.635	No lines, light evenly distributed

Name _____ Class _____ Date _____

Questions

1. a. **Interpreting Tables** If light passed from a vacuum into one of the materials listed in Table 1, which material would bend the light the most?

   _____

   _____

   _____

   b. **Inferring** Based on the index of refraction for acetone given in Table 1 and the speed of light in a vacuum, what is the speed of light through acetone?

   _____

   _____

   _____

   c. **Developing Hypotheses** Write a hypothesis to explain why an 80% sugar solution has a higher index of refraction than a 30% sugar solution.

   _____

   _____

   _____

   _____

2. a. **Interpreting Data** Based on the data in Table 2, what is the index of refraction of the unknown glass?

   _____

   _____

   b. **Drawing Conclusions** Compare the index of refraction of the unknown glass with the list of materials in Table 1. What type of material might the unknown glass be? Explain your answer.

   _____

   _____

   _____

   _____

   c. **Explaining** The researcher tested the unknown glass in immersion oils in the order listed in the table. Explain why.

   _____

   _____

   _____

   _____

Chapter 20   Electricity

Section 20.2 Electric Current and Ohm's Law
(pages 604–607)

Math Skills   *Ohm's Law*

Content and Vocabulary Support

Electric Current

The continuous flow of electric charge is an **electric current**. The unit
for measuring electric current is the ampere, or amp. It equals 1
coulomb per second. Two types of current are direct current and
alternating current. In **direct current**, the flow of charge is only in one
direction. In **alternating current**, the flow of charge regularly reverses
direction.

Resistance

As electrons move through a conducting wire, they collide with other
electrons and with ions. These collisions reduce the current in the
wire, because they convert some of the kinetic energy into thermal
energy. This opposition to the flow of charges in a material is called
resistance. The unit for measuring resistance is the ohm. A material's
thickness, length, and temperature affect its resistance.

Voltage

An electrical current depends on a difference in electrical potential
energy. Like water flowing from higher to lower heights, charges flow
spontaneously from higher to lower energy potentials. **Potential
difference** is the difference in electrical potential energy between two
places in an electric field. Potential difference is measured in joules
per coulomb, or volts. Potential difference is also called **voltage.**

Ohm's Law

According to **Ohm's Law**, the voltage (V) in a circuit equals the
product of the current (I) and the resistance (R). The law can be
expressed by the equation:

$$V = I \times R$$

This equation can be solved for current to give:

$$I = \frac{V}{R}$$

The second equation shows that increasing voltage or decreasing
resistance increases current through a circuit.

Section 20.2 Electric Current and Ohm's Law

Solved Examples

Example 1: In an electrical field, the resistance is 2 ohms and the current is 4 amps. What is the voltage?

Given: Resistance (R) = 2 ohms
Current (I) = 4 amps

Unknown: Voltage (V)

Equation: $V = I \times R$

Solution: $V = 4$ amps $\times$ 2 ohms = 8 volts

Example 2: How much current flows through a circuit in which the voltage is 9 volts and the resistance is 3 ohms?

Given: Voltage (V) = 9 volts
Resistance (R) = 3 ohms

Unknown: Current (I)

Equation: $I = \dfrac{V}{R}$

Solution: $I = \dfrac{9 \text{ volts}}{3 \text{ ohms}} = 3$ amps

Example 3: What is the resistance of a wire that has a voltage of 1.5 volts and a current of 0.5 amps?

Given: Voltage (V) = 1.5 volts
Current (I) = 0.5 amps

Unknown: Resistance (R)

Equation: $V = I \times R$

Solution: Solve the equation for R:

$$R = \frac{V}{I}$$

Substitute the given values:

$$R = \frac{1.5 \text{ volts}}{0.5 \text{ amps}} = 3.0 \text{ ohms}$$

Name _____ Class _____ Date _____

Practice Exercises

Exercise 1: Wire A has resistance of 2.0 ohms. Wire B has resistance of 2.5 ohms. Both wires have the same current. Which wire has greater voltage?

Exercise 2: What is the current in an electric field in which voltage is 12 volts and resistance is 1.5 ohms?

Exercise 3: An electric oven receives 240 volts of electricity. If it uses 32 amps of current, what is the resistance of the oven?

Exercise 4: Ellie has two wire circuits, each connected to its own 4-volt battery. One circuit has a resistance of 0.80 ohms. The other circuit carries a 4.5-amp current. Which circuit has greater resistance?

Exercise 5: Phil is trying to reduce the resistance of a 12-volt device that uses 3 amps of electricity. His goal is 3 ohms of resistance. By how many ohms does he need to reduce the resistance of the device to achieve his goal? If the resistance is lowered to 3 ohms, how many amps of current will there be?

Chapter 20 Electricity

Section 20.3 Electric Circuits

(pages 609–613)

Math **Skills** *Electric Power and Electrical Energy*

Content and Vocabulary Support

Electric Power

Recall that power is the rate of doing work. The rate at which
electrical energy is converted to another form of energy is **electric
power**. Electric power is represented by the letter P. It is the product
of current (I) and voltage (V). The equation for electric power is:

$$P = I \times V$$

Current is measured in amps (A) and voltage in volts (v). Electric
power is measured in joules per second, which are called watts (W).
Electric companies usually measure power in thousands of watts, or
kilowatts (kW).

Various appliances use different amounts of power. An appliance's
power rating tells you how much power it uses under normal
conditions. For example, an electric stove with a power rating of
6,000 watts uses 6,000 watts (6.0 kilowatts) of power, and a 4-watt
night light uses 4 watts (0.004 kilowatts) of power.

Electrical Energy

If you know the power rating of an appliance or other electrical
device, you can determine how much electrical energy it uses.
Electrical energy is represented by the letter E. It is calculated by
multiplying electric power (P) by the amount of time (t) the appliance
or device is in use. The equation for electrical energy is:

$$E = P \times t$$

Electric power is measured in kilowatts and time in hours. Electrical
energy is measured in kilowatt-hours (kWh). A kilowatt-hour equals
3.6 million joules.

Section 20.3 Electric Circuits

Solved Examples

Example 1: A microwave oven is connected to a 120-volt electric line. The microwave uses 10 amps of current. How much power does the microwave use?

Given: Voltage (V) = 120 V
Current (I) = 10 A

Unknown: Power (P)

Equation: $P = I \times V$

Solution: $P = 10 \text{ A} \times 120 \text{ V} = 1{,}200 \text{ W, or } 1.20 \text{ kW}$

Example 2: The power rating on a toaster is 1,800 W. The toaster is plugged into a 120-volt source of electricity. How many amps of current does the toaster have?

Given: Power (P) = 1,800 W
Voltage (V) = 120 V

Unknown: Current (I)

Equation: $P = I \times V$

Solution: Solve the equation for I:

$$I = \frac{P}{V}$$

Substitute the given values:

$$I = \frac{1{,}800 \text{ W}}{120 \text{ V}} = 15 \text{ A}$$

Example 3: How much electrical energy is used by a 2.3-watt camcorder running for 30 minutes?

Given: Power (P) = 2.3 W, or 0.0023 kW
Time (t) = 30 m, or 0.5 h

Unknown: Electrical energy (E)

Equation: $E = P \times t$

Solution: $E = 0.0023 \text{ kW} \times 0.5 \text{ h} = 0.00115 \text{ kWh}$

Practice Exercises

Exercise 1: How much power does a 27-amp clothes dryer use if it is connected to a 240-volt electrical source?

Exercise 2: If you operate a 2.0-kilowatt appliance for 2 hours, how much electrical energy do you use?

Exercise 3: Laci uses her 1.8-kilowatt hair dryer for 0.25 hour each day. How much electrical energy does she use each day to dry her hair?

Exercise 4: A 0.45-watt hand-held electronic game uses a 1.5-volt battery. How many amps of current does it have?

Exercise 5: Gordon's father says Gordon uses too much electrical energy by always leaving on the lights in his room. Gordon says his father uses more electrical energy when he bakes bread on Saturday, because he has the electric oven on for most of the afternoon. If Gordon leaves three 60-watt light bulbs on for 24 hours and Gordon's father uses a 7,000-watt oven for 3 hours, who uses more electrical energy?

Chapter 22 Earth's Interior

Section 22.2 Minerals

(pages 664–669)

Data ◆ Analysis *Analyzing Properties of Minerals*

Content and Vocabulary Support

Minerals and Rocks

A mineral is a naturally occurring, inorganic solid with a crystal structure and characteristic chemical composition. **Inorganic** means not produced by living things. Each mineral has a unique chemical composition and structure.

Minerals are the building blocks of rocks. A **rock** is a solid combination of minerals or mineral materials. Just a few of the thousands of known minerals make up most rocks. The most common minerals include quartz, feldspar, mica, and hornblende. Granite rock contains tiny particles of all four of these minerals. Each particle is a mineral crystal. Recall that a crystal is a solid in which atoms are arranged in a regular repeating pattern.

Properties of Minerals

Each mineral has a characteristic set of properties that result from its unique chemical composition and structure. Minerals can be identified by their properties. The properties include crystal structure, color, streak, luster, density, hardness, fracture, and cleavage.

In each type of mineral, the atoms are arranged in a particular geometric shape, or crystal structure. Each mineral always has the same crystal structure. Crystals may be shaped like prisms or cubes or have other shapes.

Some minerals can be identified by a characteristic color. For example, sulfur crystals are always yellow. However, other minerals show too much variation in color to be identified by this property alone. For example, pure quartz is clear, but quartz often has impurities that produce other colors, including violet. The color of a mineral's powder is known as its **streak**. A mineral's streak can be found by scraping the mineral against an unglazed plate. The color of the streak may be different from the color of the mineral itself. The **luster** of a mineral is the way its surface reflects light.

Density of a mineral depends on its chemical composition. Minerals made of atoms with higher atomic masses tend to have higher densities. **Hardness** is the resistance of a mineral to scratching. The **fracture** of a mineral is how the mineral breaks. **Cleavage** refers to the shapes of the pieces into which the mineral fractures. For example, mica fractures into sheets, and halite fractures into cube-shaped pieces.

Section 22.2 Minerals

Data

Hardness of minerals is ranked on a scale from 1 to 10, called the Mohs hardness scale. Table 1 shows the Mohs hardness scale with the addition of a few extra items. The scale is used by comparing unknown minerals to those in the table. For example, a mineral that scratches talc but can be scratched by gypsum has a hardness between 1 and 2.

Table 1. Modified Mohs Hardness Scale	
Hardness	Mineral or Other Item
1	Talc
2	Gypsum
2.5	Fingernail
3	Calcite
3.5	Penny
4	Fluorite
5	Apatite
5.5	Glass or steel nail
6	Orthoclase
6.5	Streak plate or good steel file
7	Quartz
8	Topaz
9	Corundum
10	Diamond

When it comes to luster, minerals can be divided into two main categories: metallic and nonmetallic. Metallic minerals look like polished metal. Nonmetallic minerals do not look like metal and fall into several additional types, some of which are listed in Table 2.

Table 2. Types of Nonmetallic Mineral Luster		
Type of Luster	Description	Examples
Adamantine	Looks extremely brilliant, much shinier than glass	Diamond, red sphalerite
Earthy	Looks dull, like soil or brick	Hematite, impure flint
Greasy	Has a faint gloss, like a coating of oil	Turquoise, pure flint
Resinous	Has a lustrous yellow or brown appearance, like resin or tree pitch	Sulfur, yellow or brown sphalerite
Silky	Looks very smooth but not shiny, like silk fabric	Asbestos, pickeringite

Name _____ Class _____ Date _____

Questions

1. a. **Interpreting Tables** A mineral called muscovite neither scratches nor is scratched by a fingernail. Based on Table 1, what is the hardness of muscovite?

   _____

   b. **Inferring** The mineral kyanite has a hardness of 7. Which minerals in Table 1 would scratch kyanite?

   _____

   _____

   c. **Applying Concepts** The hardness of the common mineral hornblende depends on its exact formula. Different hornblendes may vary by one whole point on the Mohs hardness scale. Some hornblendes can scratch glass, and some can be scratched by glass. About what range of values on the Mohs hardness scale applies to hornblendes?

   _____

2. a. **Describing** In Table 2, which type of nonmetallic mineral luster could be described as "diamond-like"?

   _____

   b. **Identifying** There are several other types of nonmetallic mineral luster in addition to those listed in Table 2. They include pearly, fibrous, and pitchy. Identify which of these three types of luster can be described as "looks like tar."

   _____

   c. **Classifying** An observer gave the following description of a mineral: "Looks like golden-brown honey or amber." Based on Table 2, what type of luster does the mineral have?

   _____

3. a. **Identifying** Based on both tables, identify a mineral that has adamantine luster and can scratch corundum.

   _____

   b. **Explaining** Explain why knowing more of a mineral's properties makes it easier to identify the mineral.

   _____

   _____

   _____

Chapter 24   Weather and Climate

Section 24.6 Predicting the Weather
(pages 774–777)

Data   Analysis   *Tracking and Forecasting Weather*

Content and Vocabulary Support

Weather Forecasting

Scientists who study weather are called **meteorologists**. Meteorologists use many technologies to help predict the weather, including Doppler radar, automated weather stations, weather satellites, and high-speed computers. Doppler radar works by bouncing radio waves off particles of precipitation. Using Doppler radar, meteorologists can track the paths of thunderstorms and potential tornadoes.

Automated weather stations are important in gathering weather data. These stations can gather information without a human observer being present. The information is transmitted as radio signals to a weather center. Weather satellites in orbit around Earth also collect information about weather, including measurements of cloud cover, humidity, temperature, and wind speed. Meteorologists use data from weather stations and satellites to form a comprehensive view of a region's weather.

With high-speed computers, meteorologists can compile and analyze the tremendous amount of weather data collected every day. Analyzing the data helps scientists make both short-term and long-term forecasts. Predicting the weather beyond a week, however, is very difficult, even with modern technology. The movement of weather systems depends on too many variables for meteorologists to forecast the weather reliably over longer periods.

Weather Maps

To help analyze weather data, meteorologists make maps that show weather patterns of different regions. The maps typically show actual or predicted temperatures and include sun or cloud symbols to indicate cloud cover. They often have symbols for rain or snow to show areas of precipitation.

Many weather maps have lines called isotherms and isobars. An **isotherm** is a line that connects points of equal air temperature. Isotherms help meteorologists see temperature patterns. An **isobar** is a line that connects points of equal air pressure. Isobars help meteorologists identify high- and low-pressure systems.

Name _____ Class _____ Date _____

Section 24.6 Predicting the Weather

Data

The table shows the average monthly rainfall for seven U.S. cities. The averages are based on monthly rainfall data collected for many decades.

Average Monthly Rainfall (mm) for Seven U.S. Cities												
City	*Jan.*	*Feb.*	*Mar.*	*Apr.*	*May*	*June*	*July*	*Aug.*	*Sep.*	*Oct.*	*Nov.*	*Dec.*
New York	83.6	78.8	98.5	93.4	106.0	84.5	105.0	104.3	91.2	83.5	106.6	92.3
Miami	51.9	52.9	62.8	82.3	150.0	227.4	152.4	197.5	215.2	177.9	79.8	47.3
Chicago	41.5	35.5	66.4	92.0	81.6	96.9	88.3	104.1	91.7	66.6	71.9	53.0
Los Angeles	67.1	59.4	45.6	21.6	3.3	0.6	0.1	2.6	5.0	7.5	39.5	39.5
Las Vegas	11.1	16.5	12.0	5.7	2.5	4.7	10.2	13.3	10.6	6.3	6.2	14.2
St. Louis	49.8	53.7	83.9	96.5	100.1	102.9	92.0	75.6	72.5	70.4	77.7	64.3
Seattle	136.6	101.3	89.9	59.1	43.1	38.1	19.3	28.9	47.7	82.0	148.0	150.1

The weather map shows air pressure (measured in pascals, Pa) over the United States on a January day. The lines on the map are isobars connecting areas of equal air pressure. The numbers on the lines show the air pressure in pascals. Adjacent isobars are 4 pascals apart. The letter "H" indicates a center of high pressure, "L" a center of low pressure, and "X" a center of either high or low pressure.

Weather Map of U.S. Showing Air Pressure

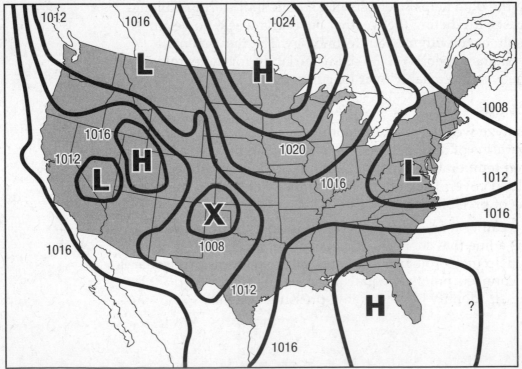

Questions

1. a. **Interpreting Tables** Which two cities have their highest average monthly rainfall in June? Which city has the lowest average monthly rainfall for any month? Which month is it?

_____

_____

_____

b. **Calculating** How much more rainfall, on average, does Los Angeles receive in January than in July? How much more rainfall, on average, does Seattle receive in January than Los Angeles receives in January?

_____

_____

_____

c. **Explaining** On one day in June several decades ago, New York City received 101.3 millimeters of rainfall. Explain how this could happen when the average monthly rainfall for New York City in June is only 84.5 millimeters.

_____

_____

_____

2. a. **Observing** What is the range of air pressures represented by the isobars on the weather map?

_____

_____

b. **Inferring** What is the air pressure for the unlabeled isobar that encircles Florida? How do you know?

_____

_____

_____

c. **Applying Concepts** Is the area labeled "X" a center of high or low air pressure? Explain your answer.

_____

_____

_____

_____

Chapter 26 Exploring the Universe

Section 26.5 The Expanding Universe
(pages 852–855)

Data **Analysis** *Hubble's Law and Hubble's Constant*

Content and Vocabulary Support

Hubble's Law

The Doppler effect can be used to determine how fast stars or galaxies are approaching or moving away from our own galaxy, the Milky Way Galaxy. When a star or galaxy is approaching us, its light shifts toward the shorter (bluer) wavelengths. When the star or galaxy is moving away, its light shifts toward the longer (redder) wavelengths. The larger the observed shift, the greater the speed of the star or galaxy.

An American astronomer named Edwin Hubble discovered that the light from most galaxies undergoes a **red shift**, or a shift toward the red wavelengths. This means that nearly all galaxies are moving farther away from the Milky Way and that the universe is expanding. Hubble also discovered that more distant galaxies are moving faster than closer galaxies. This relationship is called **Hubble's Law**. The law states that the speed at which a galaxy is moving away from our galaxy is proportional to its distance from us. In other words, the farther away a galaxy is, the redder its light appears to be.

The Big Bang Theory

Astronomers theorize that the universe came into being at a single moment, in an event called the big bang. This is called the **big bang theory**. According to this theory, all the matter and energy of the universe were at one time concentrated in an incredibly hot region smaller than the period at the end of this sentence. Then, almost 14 billion years ago, an enormous explosion occurred—the big bang. After the big bang, the universe expanded quickly and cooled down. Eventually, galaxies and solar systems formed as gravity pulled atoms together.

Scientists think that energy produced during the big bang is still traveling throughout the universe as cosmic microwave background radiation. They also think the rate of expansion of the universe may be increasing. If the rate of expansion is increasing, the universe might expand forever.

Section 26.5 The Expanding Universe

Data

Hubble estimated the speed of different galaxies, based on the degree to which their light shifted toward the red wavelengths. He found that the ratio of speed to distance for all the galaxies he studied was about the same. This ratio is now called Hubble's constant.

Distance and Speed of Selected Galaxies		
Galaxy	Distance from Milky Way Galaxy ($\times 10^6$ light-years)	Speed (km/s)
A	290	5,800
B	675	13,500
C	900	18,000
D	1,360	27,200
E	1,500	30,000

Hubble's work supports the big bang theory of the universe. Although many scientists now accept the big bang theory, they disagree about what will happen to the universe in the future. Three different models have been suggested. They are represented in the graph below. The open universe model assumes that the universe will continue expanding forever. The flat universe model assumes that expansion will eventually end but the universe will remain very large. The closed universe model assumes that the universe will eventually shrink back down to its original size.

Models of the Universe

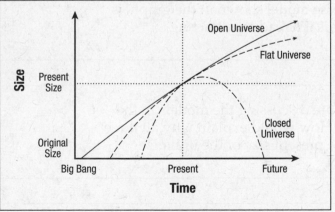

Name _____ Class _____ Date _____

Questions

1. **a. Applying Concepts** Write an equation for calculating Hubble's constant that represents the relationship between distance and speed.

   _____

   b. Calculating Use your equation to find the value of Hubble's constant, based on the values for distance and speed in the table.

   _____

   _____

   _____

   _____

   _____

   c. Problem Solving Use the value you calculated for Hubble's constant to find the distance of a galaxy moving away from the Milky Way Galaxy at a speed of 6,000 kilometers per second.

   _____

   _____

   _____

2. **a. Interpreting Graphs** According to the graph, which model of the universe assumes the big bang occurred in the most distant past?

   _____

   _____

   b. Observing In the closed universe model shown in the graph, is the universe still expanding, or is it already contracting?

   _____

   _____

   c. Communicating Assume you are discussing the models in the graph with a younger student. How would explain why all three models agree with regard to the present size of the universe?

   _____

   _____

   _____

   _____

   _____

Math Appendix

Proportions

Name _____ Class _____ Date _____

Reteaching

Proportions

A *proportion* states that two ratios are equal. To solve a proportion that contains a variable, find a value of the variable that makes the statement true. Use *cross products*.

Example 1: Solve the proportion $\frac{3}{4} = \frac{n}{20}$.

① Write the proportion. $\frac{3}{4} = \frac{n}{20}$

② Use cross products. $3 \cdot 20 = 4 \cdot n$

③ Solve. $60 = 4n$
$15 = n$

When you write a proportion, remember that matching terms in the ratios should represent the same thing.

Example 2: Minh makes bouquets having 4 roses out of 7 flowers. How many roses are there out of 14 flowers?

① Write the proportion. $\frac{4}{7} = \frac{n}{14} \frac{(roses)}{(flowers)}$

② Use cross products. $4 \cdot 14 = 7n$

③ Solve. $56 = 7n$
$8 = n$

There are 8 roses out of 14 flowers.

Solve each proportion.

1. $\frac{5}{3} = \frac{n}{6}$

   $30 =$ _____

   $n =$ _____

2. $\frac{s}{4} = \frac{7}{2}$

   $2s =$ _____

   $s =$ _____

3. $\frac{15}{12} = \frac{5}{y}$

   $15y =$ _____

   $y =$ _____

4. $\frac{5}{7} = \frac{w}{21}$

   $105 =$ _____

   $w =$ _____

5. $\frac{b}{10} = \frac{6}{15}$

   $15b =$ _____

   $b =$ _____

6. $\frac{9}{12} = \frac{3}{n}$

   $9n =$ _____

   $n =$ _____

Write a proportion for each situation. Then solve.

7. Eight out of 10 fish are trout. How many trout are there out of 40 fish?

   _____

   $w =$ _____

8. There is 1 robin for every 5 birds. How many robins are there for 15 birds?

   _____

   $b =$ _____

9. Two flowers cost $.66. How much does 1 flower cost?

   _____

   $n =$ _____

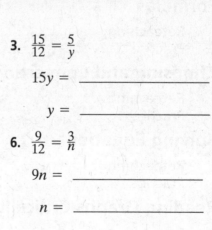

 Physical Science Math Skills and Problem Solving Workbook

Practice

- -

Solve each proportion.

1. $\frac{3}{8} = \frac{m}{16}$ _____

2. $\frac{9}{4} = \frac{27}{x}$ _____

3. $\frac{18}{6} = \frac{j}{1}$ _____

4. $\frac{b}{18} = \frac{7}{6}$ _____

5. $\frac{12}{q} = \frac{3}{4}$ _____

6. $\frac{3}{2} = \frac{15}{r}$ _____

7. $\frac{5}{x} = \frac{25}{15}$ _____

8. $\frac{80}{20} = \frac{4}{n}$ _____

Estimate the solution of each proportion.

9. $\frac{m}{25} = \frac{16}{98}$ _____

10. $\frac{7}{3} = \frac{52}{n}$ _____

11. $\frac{30}{5.9} = \frac{k}{10}$ _____

12. $\frac{2.8}{j} = \frac{1.3}{2.71}$ _____

13. $\frac{y}{12} = \frac{2.89}{4.23}$ _____

14. $\frac{5}{8} = \frac{b}{63}$ _____

15. $\frac{9}{4} = \frac{35}{d}$ _____

16. $\frac{c}{7} = \frac{28}{50}$ _____

Solve each proportion.

17. $\frac{4}{5} = \frac{b}{40}$

18. $\frac{11}{7} = \frac{88}{c}$

19. $\frac{x}{1.4} = \frac{28}{5.6}$

20. $\frac{0.99}{a} = \frac{9}{11}$

21. $\frac{42.5}{20} = \frac{x}{8}$

22. $\frac{15}{25} = \frac{7.5}{y}$

23. $\frac{16}{b} = \frac{56}{38.5}$

24. $\frac{z}{54} = \frac{5}{12}$

25. $\frac{8}{12} = \frac{e}{3}$

26. $\frac{v}{35} = \frac{15}{14}$

27. $\frac{60}{n} = \frac{12}{5}$

28. $\frac{6}{16} = \frac{9}{w}$

29. $\frac{4}{7} = \frac{r}{35}$

30. $\frac{18}{16} = \frac{27}{t}$

31. $\frac{n}{12} = \frac{12.5}{15}$

32. $\frac{27}{f} = \frac{40.5}{31.5}$

33. 5 is to 8 as 15 is to w

34. y is to 8 as 22.5 is to 10

35. 14 is to b as 28 is to 18

36. 10 is to 7 as m is to 10.5

37. 30 is to 16 as j is to 8

38. r is to 17 as 81 is to 51

Write a proportion for each situation. Then solve.

39. Jaime paid $1.29 for three ponytail holders. At that rate, what would eight ponytail holders cost her?

40. According to a label, there are 25 calories per serving of turkey lunch meat. How many calories are there in 2.5 servings?

41. Arturo paid $8 in tax on a purchase of $200. At that rate, what would the tax be on a purchase of $150?

42. Chris drove 200 mi in 4 h. At that rate, how long would it take Chris to drive 340 mi?

Reteaching

A *percent* is a ratio that compares a number to 100.

- To *write a fraction as a percent*, find the equivalent fraction with denominator 100. Write the numerator to show the percent.

$$\frac{3}{10} = \frac{3 \cdot 10}{10 \cdot 10} = \frac{30}{100}$$

- To *write a percent as a fraction*, compare the number to 100, then simplify.

$$40\% = \frac{40}{100} = \frac{2}{5}$$

- To *write a decimal as a percent*, move the decimal point two places to the right and write the % sign.

$$0.78 = 78\%$$
$$0.054 = 5.4\%$$
$$3.9 = 390\%$$

- To *write a percent as a decimal*, remove the % sign and move the decimal point two places to the left.

$$34\% = 0.34$$
$$0.9\% = 0.009$$
$$460\% = 4.6$$

Another way to change between a fraction and a percent is to use a decimal as an intermediate step.

Fraction → Decimal → Percent

$$\frac{3}{8} = 3 \div 8 = 0.375 = 37.5\%$$

Percent → Decimal → Fraction

$$250\% = 2.50 = 2\frac{50}{100} = 2\frac{1}{2}$$

Write each decimal as a percent.

1. 0.39 _____

2. 0.08 _____

3. 4.2 _____

4. 0.5 _____

5. 9 _____

6. 0.056 _____

Write each fraction as a percent.

7. $\frac{3}{4}$ _____

8. $\frac{1}{5}$ _____

9. $\frac{7}{10}$ _____

10. $\frac{5}{8}$ _____

11. $\frac{1}{4}$ _____

12. $\frac{3}{5}$ _____

Write each percent as a decimal.

13. 45% _____

14. 90% _____

15. 0.2% _____

16. 150% _____

17. 4% _____

18. 32% _____

Write each percent as a fraction in simplest form.

19. 25% _____

20. 10% _____

21. 68% _____

22. 450% _____

23. 12% _____

24. 375% _____

Practice

Write each decimal as a percent.

1. 0.95 _____   **2.** 0.06 _____   **3.** 0.004 _____   **4.** 0.27 _____

5. 0.63 _____   **6.** 0.005 _____   **7.** 1.4 _____   **8.** 2.57 _____

Choose a calculator or a paper and pencil to write each fraction as a percent. Round to the nearest tenth of a percent.

9. $\frac{4}{5}$ _____   **10.** $\frac{7}{10}$ _____   **11.** $\frac{5}{6}$ _____   **12.** $4\frac{1}{2}$ _____

13. $\frac{5}{8}$ _____   **14.** $\frac{1}{15}$ _____   **15.** $\frac{9}{25}$ _____   **16.** $1\frac{7}{8}$ _____

17. $\frac{1}{6}$ _____   **18.** $\frac{11}{12}$ _____   **19.** $\frac{1}{20}$ _____   **20.** $3\frac{9}{20}$ _____

Write each percent as a decimal.

21. 70% _____   **22.** 10% _____   **23.** 800% _____   **24.** 37% _____

25. 2.6% _____   **26.** 234% _____   **27.** 9% _____   **28.** $3\frac{1}{2}$% _____

Write each percent as a fraction in simplest form.

29. 10% _____   **30.** 47% _____   **31.** $5\frac{1}{2}$% _____   **32.** 473% _____

33. 15% _____   **34.** 92% _____   **35.** $3\frac{1}{4}$% _____   **36.** 548% _____

37. 85% _____   **38.** 42% _____   **39.** 70% _____   **40.** 150% _____

Solve.

41. There are twelve pairs of cranial nerves connected to the brain. Ten of these pairs are related to sight, smell, taste, and sound. What percent of the pairs are related to sight, smell, taste, and sound?

_____

42. If a person weighs 150 lb, then calcium makes up 3 lb of that person's weight. What percent of a person's weight does calcium make up?

_____

43. A quality control inspector found that 7 out of every 200 flashlights produced were defective. What percent of the flashlights were *not* defective?

_____

44. In 1992, 80 varieties of reptiles were on the endangered species list. Eight of these were found only in the United States. What percent of the reptiles on the endangered species list were found only in the United States?

_____

Reteaching

To add or subtract fractions and mixed numbers with unlike denominators, first rewrite the fractions using the least common denominator (LCD).

Subtract: $2\frac{3}{4} - 5\frac{1}{3}$

$$2\frac{3}{4} - 5\frac{1}{3} = \frac{11}{4} - \frac{16}{3}$$
$$= \frac{33}{12} - \frac{64}{12} \quad \leftarrow \text{The LCD is 12.}$$
$$= \frac{-31}{12} \quad \leftarrow \text{Subtract numerators.}$$
$$= -2\frac{7}{12} \quad \leftarrow \text{Simplify.}$$
$$2\frac{3}{4} - 5\frac{1}{3} = -2\frac{7}{12}$$

You can use addition or subtraction to solve equations with fractions.

Solve: $h - \frac{3}{8} = \frac{1}{6}$

$$h - \frac{3}{8} + \frac{3}{8} = \frac{1}{6} + \frac{3}{8} \quad \leftarrow \text{Add } \frac{3}{8}.$$
$$h = \frac{4}{24} + \frac{9}{24} \quad \leftarrow \text{The LCD is 24.}$$
$$h = \frac{13}{24}$$

To multiply fractions, multiply numerators, then multiply denominators.

Multiply: $\frac{7}{12} \cdot 1\frac{4}{5}$

$$\frac{7}{12} \cdot \frac{9}{5} \quad \leftarrow \text{fraction form}$$
$$\frac{7 \cdot 9}{12 \cdot 5} \quad \begin{array}{l}\leftarrow \text{Multiply numerators.}\\ \leftarrow \text{Multiply denominators.}\end{array}$$
$$\frac{63}{60} = 1\frac{3}{60} = 1\frac{1}{20} \quad \leftarrow \text{Simplify.}$$

To divide fractions, multiply by the reciprocal of the divisor.

Divide: $-3\frac{1}{8} \div \frac{2}{3}$

$$\frac{-25}{8} \div \frac{2}{3} \quad \leftarrow \text{fraction form}$$
$$\frac{-25}{8} \cdot \frac{3}{2} \quad \leftarrow \text{reciprocal of divisor}$$
$$\frac{-25 \cdot 3}{8 \cdot 2} = \frac{-75}{16} \quad \leftarrow \text{Multiply.}$$
$$= -4\frac{11}{16} \quad \leftarrow \text{Simplify.}$$

Find each sum or difference as a fraction or mixed number in simplest form.

1. $6\frac{1}{4} - 2\frac{3}{8}$

2. $\frac{5}{6} + \left(-\frac{1}{2}\right)$

3. $-4\frac{1}{3} - \left(-\frac{3}{5}\right)$

4. $\frac{1}{8} - \left(-\frac{1}{6}\right)$

5. $-1\frac{3}{8} - 4\frac{1}{12}$

6. $\frac{7}{10} + \left(-1\frac{2}{5}\right)$

Find each product or quotient. Write each answer as a fraction or mixed number in simplest form.

7. $\frac{8}{9} \cdot \left(-\frac{3}{4}\right)$

8. $-\frac{1}{2} \cdot \frac{4}{5}$

9. $-\frac{2}{3} \cdot \left(-\frac{1}{8}\right)$

10. $\frac{5}{6} \div \frac{3}{5}$

11. $-\frac{3}{8} \div \left(-\frac{1}{2}\right)$

12. $-6 \div \frac{3}{4}$

Practice

Find each sum or difference as a mixed number or fraction in simplest form.

1. $\frac{3}{4} + \frac{7}{8}$ _____

2. $-1\frac{1}{6} + 2\frac{2}{3}$ _____

3. $4\frac{1}{2} - 7\frac{7}{8}$ _____

4. $-3\frac{5}{6} - \left(-4\frac{1}{12}\right)$ _____

5. $\frac{5}{18} + \frac{7}{12}$ _____

6. $-4\frac{7}{20} + 3\frac{9}{10}$ _____

7. $5\frac{8}{21} - \left(-3\frac{1}{7}\right)$ _____

8. $1\frac{19}{24} + 2\frac{23}{20}$ _____

9. $3\frac{16}{25} - 4\frac{7}{20}$ _____

Find each product or quotient. Write each answer as a fraction or mixed number in simplest form.

10. $-\frac{1}{6} \cdot 2\frac{3}{4}$ _____

11. $\frac{3}{16} \div \left(-\frac{1}{8}\right)$ _____

12. $-\frac{31}{56} \cdot (-8)$ _____

13. $-5\frac{7}{12} \div 12$ _____

14. $-8 \div \frac{1}{4}$ _____

15. $-3\frac{1}{6} \div \left(-2\frac{1}{12}\right)$ _____

16. $8\frac{3}{4} \cdot 3\frac{7}{8}$ _____

17. $-\frac{11}{12} \div \frac{5}{6}$ _____

18. $4\frac{9}{28} \cdot (-7)$ _____

Solve each equation. Write each answer as a mixed number or as a fraction in simplest form.

19. $x + \frac{3}{8} = -\frac{1}{4}$

20. $y - \frac{1}{5} = -\frac{4}{5}$

21. $z + \left(-\frac{2}{3}\right) = -\frac{1}{6}$

_____ _____ _____

22. $m - \frac{9}{10} = \frac{1}{5}$

23. $n - 1\frac{1}{3} = -3$

24. $p + \frac{7}{12} = -\frac{1}{4}$

_____ _____ _____

25. $\frac{1}{3}a = \frac{3}{10}$

26. $-\frac{3}{4}b = 9$

27. $-\frac{7}{8}c = 4\frac{2}{3}$

_____ _____ _____

28. $\frac{5}{6}n = -3\frac{3}{4}$

29. $-\frac{3}{5}x = 12$

30. $-2\frac{2}{3}y = 3\frac{1}{3}$

_____ _____ _____

31. $\frac{7}{12}y = -2\frac{4}{5}$

32. $2\frac{1}{4}z = -\frac{1}{9}$

33. $2\frac{1}{5}d = -\frac{1}{2}$

_____ _____ _____

Reteaching

Follow the order of operations when evaluating expressions with exponents.

Example 1 Evaluate $-(3 + 1)^2 + 5 \cdot 3^2$

① Work inside grouping symbols first. $-(3 + 1)^2 + 5 \cdot 3^2 = -(4)^2 + 5 \cdot 3^2$

② Work with exponents. $= -16 + 5(9)$

- To evaluate a power, write the factors and multiply.

$$5^4 = 5 \cdot 5 \cdot 5 \cdot 5 \qquad (-2)^4 = (-2) \cdot (-2) \cdot (-2) \cdot (-2) \qquad -2^4 = -(2 \cdot 2 \cdot 2 \cdot 2)$$
$$= 625 \qquad\qquad\qquad = 16 \qquad\qquad\qquad\qquad = -16$$

③ Multiply and divide from left to right. $= -16 + 45$

④ Add and subtract from left to right. $= 29$

To evaluate a variable expression with exponents, substitute a number
for the variable and then evaluate as above.

Example 2 Evaluate $-2a^3$ for $a = 3$.
$$-2a^3 = (-2)(3)^3$$
$$= (-2)(27)$$
$$= -54$$

Write using exponents.

1. $7 \cdot 7 \cdot 7 =$ _____

2. $(-6) \cdot (-6) \cdot (-6) \cdot (-6) \cdot (-6) =$ _____

3. $10 \cdot 10 \cdot 10 \cdot 10 =$ _____

4. $1 \cdot 1 \cdot 1 \cdot 1 \cdot 1 \cdot 1 =$ _____

5. $(-8) \cdot (-8) \cdot (-8) \cdot (-8) \cdot (-8) =$ _____

6. $2 \cdot 2 \cdot 2 \cdot 2 \cdot 2 \cdot 2 \cdot 2 =$ _____

Simplify each expression.

7. $3^2 + 7 \cdot 9$ _____

8. $9 \cdot 3 - 2^3$ _____

9. $2 + (10 - 3)^2$ _____

10. $6 - 3^2 \cdot 4$ _____

Evaluate each expression for the given values of the variables.

11. $m^2 - 6; m = 4$ _____

12. $4c^3; c = 2$ _____

13. $-2k^2 + 3; k = -5$ _____

14. $2d^2 \div 6; d = 3$ _____

15. $-2n^2 - 4; n = 4$ _____

16. $3ab^2; a = -4, b = 2$ _____

Practice

Write using exponents.

1. $8 \cdot 8 \cdot 8 \cdot 8 \cdot 8$

2. $(-2)(-2)(-2)(-2)$

3. $x \cdot x \cdot x \cdot x \cdot x \cdot x$

_____

_____

_____

4. $(-3m)(-3m)(-3m)$

5. $4 \cdot t \cdot t \cdot t$

6. $(5v)(5v)(5v)(5v)(5v)$

_____

_____

_____

Write each expression as a product of the same factor.

7. a^2 _____

8. 19^3 _____

9. -6^2 _____

10. $-x^3$ _____

11. $(-5)^4$ _____

12. 4^3 _____

13. $-(10)^2$ _____

14. 20^1 _____

Simplify each expression.

15. $(-4)^2 + 10 \cdot 2$ _____

16. $-4^2 + 10 \cdot 2$ _____

17. $(5 \cdot 3)^2 + 8$ _____

18. $5 \cdot 3^2 + 8$ _____

19. $9 + (7 - 4)^2$

20. $-9 + 7 - 4^2$ _____

21. $(-6)^2 + 3^3 - 7$

22. $-6^2 + 3^3 - 7$

23. $2^3 + (8 - 5) \cdot 4 - 5^2$

_____

_____

_____

24. $(2^3 + 8) - 5 \cdot 4 - 5^2$

25. $2^3 \cdot 3 - 5 \cdot 5^2 + 8$

26. $2^3 \cdot 3 - 5(5^2 + 8)$

_____

_____

_____

Evaluate each expression for the given value.

27. $4x^2$ for $x = 3$

28. $(5b)^2$ for $b = 2$

29. $-6x^2$ for $x = 3$

30. $(-3g)^2$ for $g = 2$

_____

_____

_____

_____

Estimate the value of each expression.

31. $7 + 3q; q = 7.6$

32. $j^2 + 6; j = 4.7$

33. $2m^2 - 3m; m = 1.6$

_____

_____

_____

34. $y^2 - 19y + 16; y = 2.5$

35. $x^2 + 7x - 19; x = 4.21$

36. $v^2 + v; v = 9.8$

_____

_____

_____

37. Suppose you own a card shop. You buy one line of cards at a rate of 4 cards for $5. You plan to sell the cards at a rate of 3 cards for $5. How many cards must you sell in order to make a profit of $100.

_____

Reteaching

To write a number such as 67,000 in *scientific notation,* move the decimal point to form a number between 1 and 10. The number of places moved shows which power of 10 to use.

- Write 67,000 in scientific notation.

  6.7 is between 1 and 10. So, move the decimal point in 67,000 to the left 4 places and multiply by 10^4.

  $67,000 = 6.7 \times 10^4$

To write scientific notation in *standard form,* look at the exponent. The exponent shows the number of places and the direction to move the decimal point.

- Write 8.5×10^5 in standard form.

  The exponent is positive 5, so move the decimal point 5 places to the right.

  $8.5 \times 10^5 = 850,000$

Write each number in scientific notation.

1. 6,500

2. 65,000

3. 6,520

_____

_____

_____

4. 345

5. 29,100

6. 93,000,000

_____

_____

_____

7. 200

8. 2,300

9. 23,000

_____

_____

_____

10. 450

11. 90,000

12. 96,000

_____

_____

_____

Write each number in standard form.

13. 4×10^4 _____

14. 4×10^5 _____

15. 3.6×10^3 _____

16. 4.85×10^4 _____

17. 4.05×10^2 _____

18. 7.1×10^5 _____

19. 4×10^2 _____

20. 1.3×10^2 _____

21. 7×10^1 _____

22. 2.5×10^3 _____

23. 1.81×10^3 _____

24. 1.6×10^4 _____

25. Jupiter is on the average 7.783×10^8 kilometers from the sun. _____

Which number is greater?

26. 5×10^2 or 2×10^5 _____

27. 2.1×10^3 or 2.1×10^6 _____

28. 6×10^{10} or 3×10^9 _____

29. 3.6×10^1 or 3.6×10^3 _____

Physical Science Math Skills and Problem Solving Workbook

Practice

Write each number in scientific notation.

1. 45

2. 250

3. 90

4. 200

5. 670

6. 4,100

7. 500

8. 3,000

9. 43,200

10. 97,100

11. 38,050

12. 90,200

13. 480,000

14. 960,000

15. 8,750,000

16. 407,000

Write each number in standard form.

17. 3.1×10^1

18. 8.07×10^2

19. 4.96×10^3

20. 8.073×10^2

21. 4.501×10^4

22. 9.7×10^6

23. 8.3×10^7

24. 3.42×10^4

25. 2.86×10^5

26. 3.58×10^6

27. 8.1×10^1

28. 9.071×10^2

29. 4.83×10^9

30. 2.73×10^8

31. 2.57×10^5

32. 8.09×10^4

Order each set of numbers from least to greatest.

33. $8.9 \times 10^2, 6.3 \times 10^3, 2.1 \times 10^4, 7.8 \times 10^5$

34. $2.1 \times 10^4, 2.12 \times 10^3, 3.46 \times 10^5, 2.112 \times 10^2$

35. $8.93 \times 10^3, 7.8 \times 10^2, 7.84 \times 10^3, 8.915 \times 10^4$

Write each number in scientific notation.

36. The eye's retina contains about 130 million light-sensitive cells.

37. A mulberry silkworm can spin a single thread that measures up to 3,900 ft in length.

Reteaching

Significant figures are all the digits that are known to be accurate in a measurement. In addition and subtraction, the accuracy of the answer cannot be greater than the accuracy of the least accurate measurement.

Example 1: Add the measurements 33.78 L + 102 L + 6.901 L.

1 Identify measurement with the least accuracy.   102 L

2 Accuracy   nearest liter

In multiplication and division, the number of significant figures in the answer must be the same as the number of significant figures in the measurement with the fewest significant figures.

Example 2: Multiply 6.674 km × 1.2 km.

1 Identify measurement with fewest significant figures.   1.2 km

2 Number of significant figures   2

If an answer has more significant figures than required, round it to the correct number of significant figures. Round up if the digit after the last required significant figure is 5 or more. Round down if the digit after the last required significant figure is less than 5.

Example 3: Round 8.048 to 2 significant figures.

Round down because 4 is less than 5.   8.0

Add or subtract and express the answer in the correct number of significant figures.

1. 48 + 78.1 + 46.55 = _____   2. 99.6 g + 8 g + 36.34 g = _____

3. 98.93 s − 96.2 s = _____   4. 77.54 kg − 53.268 kg = _____

Multiply or divide and express the answer in the correct number of significant figures.

5. 0.3 × 4 = _____   6. 78 m × 1.2 m = _____

7. 33.15 s ÷ 6.9 s = _____   8. 23.97 g ÷ 6.7 mL = _____

Practice

Add or subtract and express the answer in the correct number of significant figures.

1. 33.2 m + 41 m = _____

2. 98.34 − 65.2 + 9 = _____

3. 79.63 km − 8.9 km = _____

4. 0.554 s + 0.23659 s = _____

5. 9.0 + 3.33 − 2.648 = _____

6. 932.1 g − 0.89 g = _____

7. 58.78 kL − 42 kL = _____

8. 74.3 m + 68.002 m = _____

9. 47 + 9 + 1002.3 = _____

10. 98.02 m − 6.3798 m = _____

11. 67 mm + 0.34 mm = _____

12. 2.31 nm 2 0.289 nm = _____

13. 5.4889 g − 0.2 g = _____

14. 3,338.1 L − 302.67 L = _____

15. 3 s + 2.2 s + 3.24 s = _____

16. 4.339 mL + 3.48 mL = _____

Multiply or divide and express the answer in the correct number of significant figures.

17. 3.5 m × 0.98 m = _____

18. 67.884 ÷ 9.83 = _____

19. 1.23 g × 2.5 = _____

20. 9.023 m ÷ 7.56 s = _____

21. 11.23 × 1.1131 = _____

22. 1.1 × 9.02 = _____

23. 3.35 km ÷ 2.8 s = _____

24. 1.04 km × 1.2287 km = _____

25. 99.2 ÷ 3.621 = _____

26. 12.55 g ÷ 5.6 L = _____

27. 3.6 cm × 1.2 cm = _____

28. 4.03 mm × 2.003 mm = _____

29. 9.8 ÷ 6.63 = _____

30. 3.011 m/s × 2.7 s = _____

31. 5.81 m × 0.5102 m = _____

32. 8.09 ÷ 3.556 = _____

Reteaching

You can use a *formula* to find the area of a figure.

Example: Find the area of a square with side length 1.2 m.

$A = s \cdot s$	←Write the formula.
$A = (1.2)(1.2)$	←Substitute known values.
$A = 1.44$	←Simplify.

The area of the square is 1.44 m².

Knowing how to *transform a formula* by solving for one of its variables can be useful.

Write a formula to find the width of a rectangle.

Use $A = \ell w$. Solve for w.

$$\frac{A}{\ell} = \frac{\ell w}{\ell}$$

$$\frac{A}{\ell} = w; \text{ or } w = \frac{A}{\ell}$$

Area Formulas	
Rectangle:	A = length · width $\quad A = \ell w$
Square:	A = side length · side length $\quad A = s \cdot s$
Trapezoid:	$A = \frac{1}{2}$ height (sum of bases) $\quad A = \frac{1}{2} h(b_1 + b_2)$

Find the area of each figure.

1. Square: side 3.4 ft

2. Rectangle: 6 m × 2.3 m

3. Trapezoid: $b_1 = 6$ m, $b_2 = 12$ m, $h = 4.2$ m

_____

Solve each formula for the variable indicated.

4. Solve for r.
   $d = rt$

5. Solve for ℓ.
   $A = \ell w$

6. Solve for b.
   $y = rx + b$

_____

7. Solve for t.
   $I = prt$

8. Solve for h.
   $A - bh$

9. Solve for h.
   $V = \ell wh$

_____

Use the formula $d = rt$ to find each of the following.

10. time for $d = 500$ miles and $r = 50$ mi/h _____

11. rate for $d = 52.5$ miles and $t = 1.5$ hour _____

12. time for $d = 75$ km and $r = 25$ km/h _____

Physical Science Math Skills and Problem Solving Workbook

Name _____ Class _____ Date _____

Practice

Find the area and the perimeter of each figure.

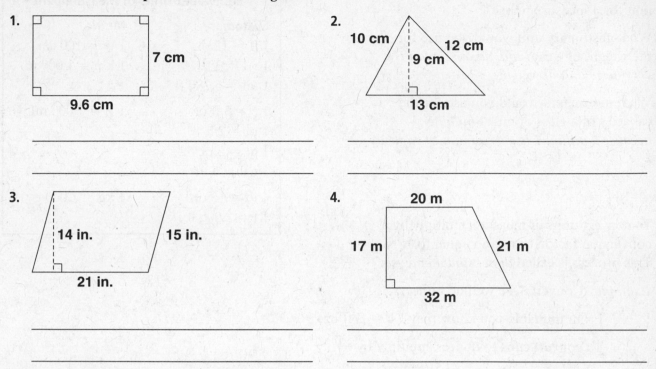

1.

7 cm

9.6 cm

_____

_____

2.

10 cm   12 cm
9 cm

13 cm

_____

_____

3.

14 in.   15 in.

21 in.

_____

_____

4.

20 m

17 m   21 m

32 m

_____

_____

Write an equation to find the solution for each problem. Solve the equation. Then give the solution for the problem.

5. The Kents left home at 7:00 A.M. and drove to their parents' house 400 mi away. They arrived at 3:00 P.M. What was their average speed?

_____

6. An airplane flew for 4 h 30 min at an average speed of 515 mi/h. How far did it fly?

_____

7. Marcia rowed her boat 18 mi downstream at a rate of 12 mi/h. How long did the trip take?

_____

In Exercises 8–11, use the formula $F = \frac{9}{5}C + 32$ or $C = \frac{5}{9}(F - 32)$ to find a temperature in either degrees Fahrenheit, °F, or degrees Celsius, °C.

8. What is the temperature in degrees Fahrenheit when it is 0°C?

_____

9. What is the temperature in degrees Fahrenheit when it is 100°C?

_____

10. What is the temperature in degrees Celsius when it is −4°F?

_____

11. What is the temperature in degrees Celsius when it is 77°F?

_____

Name _____ Class _____ Date _____

Reteaching

Sometimes you must select the appropriate unit for a measurement.

What customary unit would you use for the weight of a car? *ton, because a ton is a very large unit of weight*

What metric unit would you use for the capacity of a glass of milk? *milliliter, because a milliliter is a small unit of capacity*

Equivalent Units of Measurement	
Customary	**Metric**
1 ft = 12 in.	1 m = 100 cm
1 yd = 3 ft	1 km = 1,000 m
1 mi = 5,280 ft	
1 c = 8 fl oz	1 L = 1,000 mL
1 pt = 2 c	
1 qt = 2 pt	
1 gal = 4 qt	
1 lb = 16 oz	1 kg = 1,000 g
1 t = 2,000 lb	

To convert units of measure, multiply by a conversion factor, or a ratio equal to 1. This process is called *dimensional analysis*.

Example: Convert 4.5 c to fluid ounces.

From the table you know that **1 c = 8 fl oz.**

To convert cups to ounces, multiply by $\frac{8 \text{ fl oz}}{1 \text{ c}}$

$4.5 \text{ c} = \frac{4.5 \text{ c}}{1} \cdot \frac{8 \text{ fl oz}}{1 \text{ c}} = \frac{(4.5)(8) \text{ fl oz}}{1} = 36 \text{ fl oz}$

So, 4.5 cups equals 36 fluid ounces.

Choose an appropriate customary unit.

1. weight of a peach

   _____

2. capacity of a pitcher of lemonade

   _____

3. length of a crayon

   _____

Choose an appropriate metric unit.

4. distance to Mexico City

   _____

5. mass of a hummingbird

   _____

6. capacity of a jug of milk

   _____

Use dimensional analysis to convert each measure.

7. 48 in. = _?_ ft

   _____

8. 8,400 cm = _?_ m

   _____

9. 6 km = _?_ m

   _____

Use compatible numbers to find a reasonable estimate.

10. 15 qt is about _?_ c.

    _____

11. 32,688 g is about _?_ kg.

    _____

12. 88 oz is about _?_ lb.

    _____

Physical Science Math Skills and Problem Solving Workbook

Practice

Choose an appropriate unit.

1. length of a stapler

_____

2. weight of a cookie

_____

3. capacity of a teakettle

_____

4. height of a door

_____

5. distance to the moon

_____

6. weight of a jet aircraft

_____

Choose an appropriate metric unit.

7. mass of a cat

_____

8. length of a playground

_____

9. capacity of a test tube

_____

10. length of an insect

_____

11. capacity of a bathtub

_____

12. mass of a coin

_____

Use dimensional analysis to convert each measure. Round answers to the nearest hundredth where necessary.

13. 56 in. = _?_ ft

_____

14. 240 d = _?_ h

_____

15. 4 gal = _?_ pt

_____

16. 0.75 d = _?_ h

_____

17. 2.25 t = _?_ lb

_____

18. 84 ft = _?_ yd

_____

19. 0.25 d = _?_ min

_____

20. 18 d = _?_ h

_____

21. 0.01 t = _?_ oz

_____

Use dimensional analysis to solve each problem.

22. At one time, trains were not permitted to go faster than 12 mi/h. How many yards per minute is this?

_____

23. A mosquito can fly at 0.6 mi/h. How many inches per second is this?

_____

24. An Arctic tern flew 11,000 miles in 115 days. How many feet per minute did the bird average?

_____

25. A sneeze can travel up to 100 mi/h. How many feet per second is this?

_____

Use compatible numbers to find a reasonable estimate.

26. 118 in. is about _?_ ft.

_____

27. 3,540 seconds is about _?_ hours.

_____

Reteaching

Combining terms can help solve equations.

Solve: $5n + 6 + 3n = 22$

$5n + 3n + 6 = 22$ ← Commutative Property

$8n + 6 = 22$

$8n + 6 - 6 = 22 - 6$

$8n = 16$

$\frac{8n}{8} = \frac{16}{8}$

$n = 2$

Check: $5n + 6 + 3n = 22$

$5(2) + 6 + 3(2) \stackrel{?}{=} 22$

$22 = 22$ ✔

When an equation has a variable on both sides, add or subtract to get the variable on one side.

Solve: $-6m + 45 = 3m$

$-6m + 6m + 45 = 3m + 6m$ ← Add 6m to each side.

$45 = 9m$

$\frac{45}{9} = \frac{9m}{9}$

$5 = m$

Check: $-6m + 45 = 3m$

$-6(5) + 45 \stackrel{?}{=} 3(5)$

$15 = 15$ ✔

Solve each equation. Check the solution.

1. $a - 4a = 36$

$a = $ _____

2. $3b - 5 - 2b = 5$

$b = $ _____

3. $5n + 4 - 8n = -5$

$n = $ _____

4. $12k + 6 = 10$

$k = $ _____

5. $3(x - 4) = 15$

$x = $ _____

6. $y - 8 + 2y = 10$

$y = $ _____

7. $3(s - 10) = 36$

$s = $ _____

8. $-15 = p + 4p$

$p = $ _____

9. $2g + 3g + 5 = 0$

$g = $ _____

10. $6c + 4 - c = 24$

$c = $ _____

11. $3(x - 2) = 15$

$x = $ _____

12. $4y + 9 - 7y = -6$

$y = $ _____

13. $4(z - 2) + z = -13$

$z = $ _____

14. $24 = -2(b - 3) + 8$

$b = $ _____

15. $17 = 3(g + 3) - g$

$g = $ _____

16. $5(k - 4) = 4 - 3k$

$k = $ _____

17. $8 - m - 3m = 16$

$m = $ _____

18. $6n + n + 14 = 0$

$n = $ _____

19. $7(p + 1) = 9 - p$

$p = $ _____

20. $36 = 4(q - 5)$

$q = $ _____

21. $25 + 2t = 5(t + 2)$

$t = $ _____

Physical Science Math Skills and Problem Solving Workbook

Name _____ Class _____ Date _____

Practice

• •

Solve each equation. Check the solution.

1. $2(2.5b - 9) + 6b = -7$

_____

2. $12y = 2y + 40$

_____

3. $6(c + 4) = 4c - 18$

_____

4. $0.7w + 16 + 4w = 27.28$

_____

5. $24 = -6(m + 1) + 18$

_____

6. $0.5m + 6.4 = 4.9 - 0.1m$

_____

7. $7k - 8 + 2(k + 12) = 52$

_____

8. $14b = 16(b + 12)$

_____

9. $4(1.5c + 6) - 2c = -9$

_____

10. $7y = y - 42$

_____

11. $9(d - 4) = 5d + 8$

_____

12. $0.5n + 17 + n = 20$

_____

13. $20 = -4(f + 6) + 14$

_____

14. $12j = 16(j - 8)$

_____

15. $0.7p + 4.6 = 7.3 - 0.2p$

_____

16. $9a - 4 + 3(a - 11) = 23$

_____

17. $6(f + 5) = 2f - 8$

_____

18. $15p = 6(p - 9)$

_____

19. $0.5t + 4.1 = 5.7 - 0.3t$

_____

20. $9q - 14 + 3(q - 8) = 7$

_____

21. A banquet is planned for 50 people. The caterer charges $1,500 for the food. How much is that per person? Write an equation and solve.

_____

22. Stephanie is six years old. She is one year older than one-sixth the age of her mother. How old is Stephanie's mother? Write an equation and solve.

_____

Name _____ Class _____ Date _____

Reteaching

Two important factors in determining whether a graph gives a correct impression of data are:

- how the scale is chosen and

- whether the entire scale is shown.

The data at the right can be shown in a bar graph.

Countries with Most Universities (2000)	
India	7,513
United States	3,559

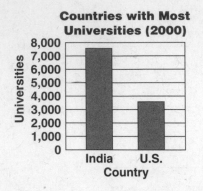

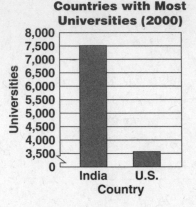

In the first graph, the scale is in multiples of 1,000. The entire scale from 0 through 8,000 is shown. The graph accurately compares the numbers of universities in the two countries.

In the second graph, the scale is in multiples of 500. There is a break in the vertical scale. The graph gives a misleading comparison between the two countries.

Use the bar graphs above for Exercises 1–4.

1. From which graph is it easier to tell that India has about twice the number of universities as the United States?

   _____

2. In the second graph, about how many times the number of U.S. universities does India *appear* to have?

   _____

3. Which graph makes it easier to estimate the number of universities in each country? Why?

   _____

   _____

   _____

4. Why does the second graph give a misleading impression of the data?

   _____

   _____

   _____

Practice

Use the graph below for Exercises 1–5.

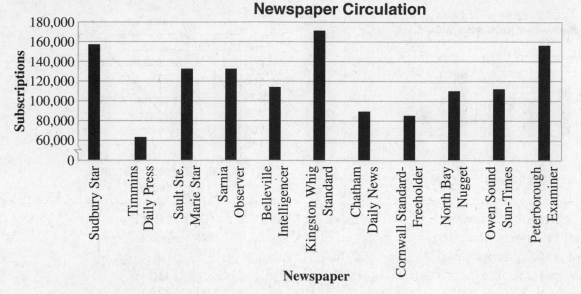

Newspaper Circulation

1. Which newspaper appears to have twice the circulation of *The Cornwall Standard-Freeholder*? _____

2. Which newspaper actually has about twice the circulation of *The Cornwall Standard-Freeholder*? _____

3. *Belleville Intelligencer* appears to have about how many times the circulation of *Chatham Daily News*? _____

4. Explain why the graph gives a misleading visual impression of the data.

   _____

   _____

5. Redraw the graph to give an accurate impression of the data.

Reteaching

Bar graphs are useful for comparing sets of data.

Line graphs and multiple line graphs show how data change over time. Line graphs help you see a trend.

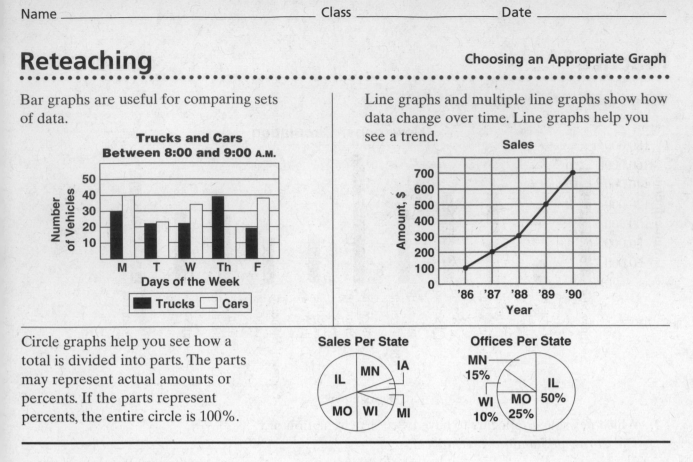

Circle graphs help you see how a total is divided into parts. The parts may represent actual amounts or percents. If the parts represent percents, the entire circle is 100%.

Decide which type of graph would be the most appropriate for the data: *circle graph, line graph, multiple line graph,* **or** *double bar graph.* **Explain your choice.**

1. two classes' test scores over a school year

   _____

2. how a club spends its money

   _____

3. the numbers of boys and the numbers of girls who use the playground each day for one week

   _____

4. the percents of chemical elements in seawater

   _____

5. a company's profit

   _____

Practice

Use the graph to the right for Exercises 1 and 2.

1. The bar graph shows the number of tickets a movie house sold each month last year. They want to look at last year's sales trend. Which type of graph would be more appropriate for the data?

   _____

2. Draw the graph.

Number of Tickets Sold

Decide which type of graph would be the most appropriate for the data. Explain your choice.

3. sizes of U.S. farms from 1950 to 2000

   _____

4. lengths of rivers

   _____

5. height versus weight of students in a class

   _____

6. the way a family budgets its income

   _____

Answers For Reteaching

Reteaching Proportions (p. 106)

1. $3n$; 10   2. 28; 14   3. 60; 4   4. $7w$; 15
5. 60; 4   6. 36; 4   7. $\frac{8}{10} = \frac{n}{40}$; 32 trout
8. $\frac{1}{5} = \frac{n}{15}$; 3 robins   9. $\frac{2}{0.66} = \frac{1}{n}$; $.33

Reteaching Fractions, Decimals, and Percents (p. 108)

1. 39%   2. 8%   3. 420%   4. 50%
5. 900%   6. 5.6%   7. 75%   8. 20%
9. 70%   10. 62.5%   11. 25%   12. 60%
13. 0.45   14. 0.9   15. 0.002   16. 1.5
17. 0.04   18. 0.32   19. $\frac{1}{4}$ 20. $\frac{1}{10}$
21. $\frac{17}{25}$ 22. $4\frac{1}{2}$ 23. $\frac{3}{25}$ 24. $3\frac{3}{4}$

Reteaching Working with Fractions (p. 110)

1. $3\frac{7}{8}$ 2. $\frac{1}{3}$ 3. $-3\frac{11}{15}$ 4. $\frac{7}{24}$ 5. $-5\frac{11}{24}$ 6. $\frac{-7}{10}$
7. $\frac{-2}{3}$ 8. $\frac{-2}{5}$ 9. $\frac{1}{12}$

Reteaching Powers and Exponents (p. 112)

1. 7^3 2. $(-6)^5$ 3. 10^4 4. 1^6 5. $(-8)^5$
6. 2^7 7. 72   8. 19   9. 51   10. -30
11. 10   12. 32   13. -47 14. 3   15. -36
16. -48

Reteaching Scientific Notation (p. 114)

1. 6.5×10^3 2. 6.5×10^4 3. 6.52×10^3
4. 3.45×10^2 5. 2.91×10^4 6. 9.3×10^7
7. 2×10^2 8. 2.3×10^3 9. 2.3×10^4
10. 4.5×10^2 11. 9×10^4 12. 9.6×10^4
13. 40,000   14. 400,000   15. 3,600
16. 48,500   17. 405   18. 710,000
19. 400   20. 130   21. 70   22. 2,500
23. 1,810   24. 16,000   25. 778,300,000 km
26. 2×10^5 27. 2.1×10^6
28. 6×10^{10} 29. 3.6×10^3

Reteaching Significant Figures (p. 116)

1. 173   2. 144g   3. 2.7 s   4. 24.27 kg
5. 1   6. 94 m^2 7. 4.8 s   8. 3.6 g/mL

Reteaching Formulas (p. 118)

1. $A = 11.56 \text{ ft}^2$ 2. $A = 13.8 \text{ m}^2$ 3. $A = 37.8 \text{ m}^2$
4. $r = \frac{d}{t}$ 5. $\ell = \frac{A}{w}$ 6. $b = y - rx$
7. $t = \frac{I}{pr}$ 8. $h = \frac{A}{b}$ 9. $h = \frac{V}{\ell w}$
10. 10 h   11. 35 mi/h   12. 3 h

Reteaching Choosing and Converting Units (p. 120)

1. ounce   2. quart   3. inch   4. kilometer
5. gram   6. liter   7. 4   8. 84
9. 6,000   10. 60   11. 33   12. 6

Reteaching Solving Equations (p. 122)

1. -12 2. 10   3. 3   4. $\frac{1}{3}$ 5. 9
6. 6   7. 22   8. -3 9. -1 10. 4
11. 7   12. 5   13. -1 14. -5 15. 4
16. 3   17. -2 18. -2 19. $\frac{1}{4}$ 20. 14
21. 5

Reteaching Understanding Graphs (p. 124)

1. the first graph   2. about 9 times
3. The second graph; since the scale is smaller, the bars can be read more accurately.
4. By using the break, most of the bar for the United States has been left out.

Reteaching Choosing an Appropriate Graph (p. 126)

1. multiple line graph; shows changes in two sets of data over time
2. circle graph; shows how the club's budget is divided into parts
3. double bar graph; compares two sets of data
4. circle graph; shows how 100% is divided into parts
5. line graph; shows change over time

Answers for Practice

Practice Proportions (p. 107)

1. 6 **2.** 12 **3.** 3 **4.** 21 **5.** 16
6. 10 **7.** 3 **8.** 1
9–16. Sample answers are given. **9.** 4 **10.** 21
11. 50 **12.** 5.6 **13.** 9 **14.** 40 **15.** 16
16. 4 **17.** 32 **18.** 56 **19.** 7 **20.** 1.21
21. 17 **22.** 12.5 **23.** 11 **24.** 22.5 **25.** 2
26. 37.5 **27.** 25 **28.** 24 **29.** 20 **30.** 24
31. 10 **32.** 21 **33.** 24 **34.** 18 **35.** 9
36. 15 **37.** 15 **38.** 27 **39.** $\frac{1.29}{3} = \frac{x}{8}$; \$3.44
40. $\frac{25}{1} = \frac{x}{2.5}$; 62.5 calories **41.** $\frac{8}{200} = \frac{x}{150}$; \$6
42. $\frac{200}{4} = \frac{340}{x}$; 6.8 h, or 6 h 48 min

Practice Fractions, Decimals, and Percents (p. 109)

1. 95% **2.** 6% **3.** 0.4% **4.** 27% **5.** 63%
6. 0.5% **7.** 140% **8.** 257% **9.** 80% **10.** 70%
11. 83.3% **12.** 450% **13.** 62.5% **14.** 6.7% **15.** 36%
16. 187.5% **17.** 16.7% **18.** 91.7% **19.** 5% **20.** 345%
21. 0.7 **22.** 0.10 **23.** 8.0 **24.** 0.37 **25.** 0.026
26. 2.34 **27.** 0.09 **28.** 0.035 **29.** $\frac{1}{10}$ **30.** $\frac{47}{100}$
31. $\frac{11}{200}$ **32.** $4\frac{73}{100}$ **33.** $\frac{3}{20}$ **34.** $\frac{23}{25}$ **35.** $\frac{13}{400}$
36. $5\frac{12}{25}$ **37.** $\frac{17}{20}$ **38.** $\frac{21}{50}$ **39.** $\frac{7}{10}$ **40.** $1\frac{1}{2}$
41. 83.3% **42.** 2% **43.** 96.5% **44.** 10%

Practice Working with Fractions (p. 111)

1. $1\frac{5}{8}$ **2.** $1\frac{1}{2}$ **3.** $-3\frac{3}{8}$ **4.** $\frac{1}{4}$ **5.** $\frac{31}{36}$
6. $\frac{-9}{20}$ **7.** $8\frac{11}{21}$ **8.** $4\frac{113}{120}$ **9.** $\frac{-71}{100}$ **10.** $\frac{-11}{24}$
11. $-1\frac{1}{2}$ **12.** $4\frac{3}{7}$ **13.** $\frac{-67}{144}$ **14.** -32 **15.** $1\frac{13}{25}$
16. $33\frac{29}{32}$ **17.** $-1\frac{1}{10}$ **18.** $-30\frac{1}{4}$ **19.** $\frac{-5}{8}$ **20.** $\frac{-3}{5}$
21. $\frac{1}{2}$ **22.** $1\frac{1}{10}$ **23.** $-1\frac{2}{3}$ **24.** $\frac{-5}{6}$ **25.** $\frac{9}{10}$
26. -12 **27.** $-5\frac{1}{3}$ **28.** $-4\frac{1}{2}$ **29.** -20 **30.** $-1\frac{1}{4}$
31. $-4\frac{4}{5}$ **32.** $\frac{-4}{81}$ **33.** $\frac{-5}{22}$

Practice Powers and Exponents (p. 113)

1. 8^5 **2.** $(-2)^4$ **3.** x^6 **4.** $(-3m)^3$
5. $4t^3$ **6.** $(5v)^5$ **7.** $a \cdot a$ **8.** $19 \cdot 19 \cdot 19$
9. $-(6)(6)$ **10.** $-(x)(x)(x)$
11. $(-5)(-5)(-5)(-5)$ **12.** $4 \cdot 4 \cdot 4$
13. $-(10)(10)$ **14.** 20 **15.** 36
16. 4 **17.** 233 **18.** 53 **19.** 18
20. -18 **21.** 56 **22.** -16 **23.** -5
24. -29 **25.** -93 **26.** -141 **27.** 36
28. 100 **29.** -54 **30.** 36 **31.** 29.8
32. 28.09 **33.** 0.32 **34.** -25.25 **35.** 28.1941
36. 105.84 **37.** 240 cards

Practice Scientific Notation (p. 115)

1. 4.5×10^1 **2.** 2.5×10^2 **3.** 9×10^1
4. 2×10^2 **5.** 6.7×10^2 **6.** 4.1×10^3
7. 5×10^2 **8.** 3×10^3 **9.** 4.32×10^4
10. 9.71×10^4 **11.** 3.805×10^4 **12.** 9.02×10^4
13. 4.8×10^5 **14.** 9.6×10^5 **15.** 8.75×10^6
16. 4.07×10^5 **17.** 31 **18.** 807
19. 4,960 **20.** 807.3 **21.** 45,010
22. 9,700,000 **23.** 83,000,000 **24.** 34,200
25. 286,000 **26.** 3,580,000 **27.** 81
28. 907.1 **29.** 4,830,000,000 **30.** 273,000,000
31. 257,000 **32.** 80,900
33. $8.9 \times 10^2, 6.3 \times 10^3, 2.1 \times 10^4, 7.8 \times 10^5$
34. $2.112 \times 10^2, 2.12 \times 10^3, 2.1 \times 10^4, 3.46 \times 10^5$
35. $7.8 \times 10^2, 7.84 \times 10^3, 8.93 \times 10^3, 8.915 \times 10^4$
36. 1.3×10^8 cells
37. 3.9×10^3 ft

Practice Significant Figures (p. 117)

1. 74 m **2.** 42 **3.** 70.7 km **4.** 0.791 s
5. 9.7 **6.** 931.2 g **7.** 17 kL **8.** 142.3 m
9. 1058 **10.** 91.64 m **11.** 67 mm **12.** 2.02 mm
13. 5.3 g **14.** 3035.4 L **15.** 8 s **16.** 7.82 mL
17. 3.4 m **18.** 6.91 **19.** 3.1 g **20.** 1.19 m/s
21. 12.50 **22.** 9.9 **23.** 1.2 km/s **24.** 1.28 km^2
25. 27.4 **26.** 2.2 g/L **27.** 4.3 cm^2 **28.** 8.07 nm^2
29. 1.5 **30.** 8.1 m **31.** 2.96 m^2 **32.** 2.28

Practice Formulas (p. 119)

1. $P = 2l + 2w; A = l \cdot w; P = 33.2$ cm; $A = 67.2$ cm^2
2. $P = a + b + c; A = \frac{1}{2}b \cdot h; P = 35$ cm; $A = 58.5$ cm^2
3. $P = 2a + 2b; A = bh; P = 72$ in.; $A = 294$ in.^{2}
4. $P = a + b + c + d; A = \frac{1}{2}h(b_1 + b_2); P = 90$ m; $A = 442$ m^2
5. $8s = 400; 50$ mi/h **6.** $4.5 \times 515 = d; 2,317.5$ mi
7. $12t = 18; 1.5$ h **8.** $32°$F
9. $212°$F **10.** $-20°$C **11.** $25°$C

Answers for Practice (continued)

Practice Choosing and Converting Units (p. 121)

1. inch   **2.** ounce   **3.** quart   **4.** foot
5. mile   **6.** ton   **7.** kilogram   **8.** meter
9. milliliter   **10.** centimeter   **11.** liter
12. gram   **13.** 4.67   **14.** 5,760   **15.** 32
16. 18   **17.** 4,500   **18.** 28   **19.** 360
20. 432   **21.** 320   **22.** 352 yd/min
23. 10.56 in./s   **24.** 350.72 ft/min   **25.** 146.67 ft/s
26. 10   **27.** 1

Practice Solving Equations (p. 123)

1. 1   **2.** 4   **3.** −21   **4.** 2.4   **5.** −2
6. −2.5   **7.** 4   **8.** −96   **9.** −8.25   **10.** −7
11. 11   **12.** 2   **13.** −7.5   **14.** 32   **15.** 3
16. 5   **17.** −9.5   **18.** −6   **19.** 2   **20.** 3.75
21. $50x = \$1,500$; \$30.00 per person
22. $6 = \frac{1}{6}x + 1$; 30 years old

Practice Understanding Graphs (p. 125)

Sample answers for Exercises 1–5:
1. *Sault Ste. Marie Star* or *Sarina Observer*
2. *Kingston Whig Standard*   **3.** 1.5
4. The graph begins at 60,000. This makes the values appear farther apart than they are.
5.

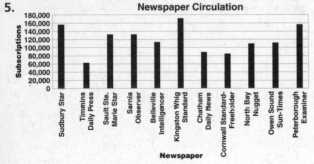

Practice Choosing an Appropriate Graph (p. 127)

1. a line graph
2.

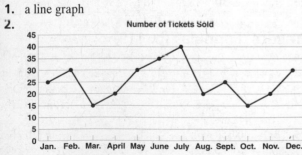

3. line graph, shows change over time
4. bar graph, compares quantities
5. scatter plot, shows a relationship between sets of data
6. circle graph, compares parts of a whole